ADVANCE PRAISE FOR LOW

"It's rare for a book to create the feeling of meeting a long-lost kindred spirit, but *Low Road Forever* does so perfectly. Engaging and genuine, Tara's voice is one that understands the importance of merging critical thought with excellent conversation while not wasting words. I'll be livid if she doesn't write another book tomorrow."

–ANNE T. DONAHUE, author of *Nobody Cares*

"*Low Road Forever* is part volcano and part manifesto. Each essay has its own velocity and force and each offers a bullshit-free understanding of the importance of our crucial things: art and culture and protest and feminism while also laying a trail that starts out rural and lands in an uncontrollable, queer, and unapologetic manifestation of selfhood in all its glory.... A book that will keep you bright and righteous with so much heart, there'll be no stopping your own from flaring."

–SUE GOYETTE, Governor General's Award–nominated author, and Poet Laureate of Halifax

"Wry. Unflinching. Prescient. These are some of the words that came to mind as I was reading Tara Thorne's essays in *Low Road Forever*. Thorne's voice is a beacon. Don't be fooled by her self-deprecating tone. This is a writer who moves with ease and insight across all topics that sustain her interest or ire. Readers will laugh, shudder, and learn from Thorne's keen eye."

–ERIN WUNKER, award-winning author of *Notes from a Feminist Killjoy*

"*Low Road Forever* is all confessions and vulnerability. It's permission to change your mind and like what you like. Tara Thorne pulls back the curtain on pretension, revealing unwavering support for women. An affirming read for this recovering 'not like the other girls.'"

–REBECCA THOMAS, author of *I place you into the fire*

"For twenty years, Tara Thorne has offered her frank and refreshing perspective on arts and culture in Halifax and beyond. In *Low Road Forever*, she offers both a compendium of the kind of charming, laugh-out-loud writing her readers are used to as well as a deeper look at the person behind the persona. Inviting us into her singular perspective, Thorne creates an honest, irreverent, sometimes darkly painful portrayal of what it is to be human. On every page, her wit, intelligence, and relentless sense of humour shine through."

–RYAN TURNER, author of *Half Sisters & Other Stories*

"However good you think this book is going to be—it's better. Teeming with the signature wit, rage, and humour that makes Tara Thorne a local fucking treasure, it's as funny and engaging as I expected. What I did not expect was how vulnerable and intimate these essays would be. I want to hug this book to my chest, let its weight hold me down as I walk into the sea. There is no one who crafts a final paragraph like Tara, and every single time the wit, the wisdom, punched me in the gut. I'm not over it. I'll never be over it."

–LINDSAY GLOADE-RAINING BIRD, journalist and host of *Book Me!* podcast

"Tara Thorne is soon to be the leader of a devoted cult follow-ing. Only Thorney could call Toronto and Vancouver the 'dollar store versions of New York and Los Angeles,' tell the reader to go fuck themselves, and still find herself engrained in our hearts forever. This book is real. Hilarious. Addictive. REFRESHING. and fun as hell! We are charmed. And we want to send her a fancy taxi."
—JENN GRANT, musician

LOW ROAD FOREVER

& OTHER ESSAYS

TARA THORNE

NIMBUS
PUBLISHING
— NIMBUS.CA —

Nimbus Publishing Limited
3660 Strawberry Hill St, Halifax, NS, B3K 5A9
(902) 455-4286 nimbus.ca

Printed and bound in Canada

Parts of "The Man-hating Dyke" originally appeared in the April 2021 issue of *Workprint*, the official newsletter of the Atlantic Filmmakers Co-operative.

Parts of "Independent Christmas" originally appeared in the December 3, 2015, issue of *The Coast*.

Editor: Stephanie Domet
Editor for the press: Whitney Moran
Cover Design: Megan Fildes
NB1584

Library and Archives Canada Cataloguing in Publication

Title: Low road forever : & other essays / Tara Thorne.
Names: Thorne, Tara, author.
Identifiers: Canadiana (print) 2022026211X | Canadiana (ebook) 20220262136 |
ISBN 9781774711194 (softcover) | ISBN 9781774711750 (EPUB)
Subjects: LCGFT: Essays.
Classification: LCC PS8639.H6578 L69 2022 | DDC C814/.6—dc23

Canada Council   Conseil des arts
for the Arts   du Canada

Nimbus Publishing acknowledges the financial support for its publishing activities from the Government of Canada, the Canada Council for the Arts, and from the Province of Nova Scotia. We are pleased to work in partnership with the Province of Nova Scotia to develop and promote our creative industries for the benefit of all Nova Scotians.

For Alicia,
the longest-suffering person
in this car.

CONTENTS

HERE'S THE FUCKING BOOK
(AN INTRODUCTION)

If you're reading this you're probably a friend of mine, which means you know my deal, which means you've been made to feel you have to pay money for thoughts I have definitely loudly expressed in your vicinity at some juncture. I appreciate your curiously continuous support.

Leaving/being shoved out of journalism, to the surprise of no journalist past or present, quickly became the best thing that ever happened to me. I was fired on August 10, 2020, and by Labour Day I had received funding to make my feature film, the (paid!) opportunity to host a new podcast, and an invitation to write this book.

Though I was on the radio for fifteen years, I don't listen to it; though I have hosted or co-hosted four podcasts, I don't subscribe to a single one; though I have written this book, I do not read books. In my youth I was a voracious reader of fiction—I grew up in the country and the internet wasn't invented until I was in high school, so reading books was the one thing I had to do—and an English major in university, but once I became a working journalist reading books just fell away. I held onto multiple magazine subscriptions until about 2015, but those too are now a thing of the past. I was always reading, for my job.

Over the years people would sometimes ask if I had a book in me and the answer was always no, because if I was going to make shit up I would do it in screenplay form. In Halifax, screen-writing is not a common profession and it's hard to relate to, so that admission would usually stop the conversation dead. I always considered the question a compliment, but a laughable one. *Me?!* Write a *book?!* About *what?!* When this book offer came, in the wake of that awful August, it felt like another win. The deadline was far down the road, after the movie—a lifelong dream—finished. Someone wanted to pay me for my opinions, the same ones that just got me fired? It would be totally fine, probably! Of course I'd write the book.

The acquisition announcement dropped the same day I learned I'd lost my union grievance with CBC, a triumph of a shitty old door closing while a significantly more appealing window opened. But if you are not a friend of mine—or even if you're an enemy; a hate-read is still a read!—here's the basic deal: I have lived a mostly unremarkable and occasionally thrilling life in Halifax, Nova Scotia, where I spent nearly two decades as an arts journalist. First with *The Coast*, the city's weekly alternative newspaper, where I got hired at twenty, did a handful of jobs, and left with little grace at thirty-nine. I also appeared weekly as an entertainment columnist and critic on the radio morning shows at CBC Halifax, then Saint John, then Moncton—for a whole decade I had to keep my New Brunswick thoughts (negative) to myself—until the summer of 2020, when I was fired for tweeting a single joke about the then-premier of Nova Scotia's son's sex life.

(I am not classy enough not to say a real fuck-you to those who thought they had cancelled me.) It earned me the most likes and comments I'd ever received on any online post. People were stoked about the book. I focused on the movie.

I've never believed in the adage that "the easiest thing to do is not write"; even though I am a classic procrastinator I am also very good with deadlines and writing can be challenging, but it's not hard for me. Yet I walked around town for what felt like years (it was months) with The Book looming. People asked me about it constantly, because A Book is the most respectable—to normies—of all the opportunities I received in the wake of my termination. "We don't mention The Book," was my stock response, as I mimed slashing my own throat.

Writing this collection has been the hardest thing I've ever done, even though the entire thing is literally just my thoughts and opinions about pop culture, music, feminism, and things I hate. It required no interviews, little research, and zero world-building. Yet I did everything I could to avoid it: I got a kitten. I made a record. I released that record. I made the feature. I wrote two more full-length screenplays and staged one of them live. I coordinated two Halifax Independent Filmmakers Festivals.

Still, The Book shadowed every day of my life. People eventually stopped asking me about it because my responses had become so ornery.

When Joan Didion died in December 2021, it stirred up the usual discourse about whether essays are "as good" as prose, as if so many vaunted novels are not just the author's personal stories with some names changed. I am not a literary snob—I don't have the background—so I don't have an opinion. Some people are very good at making shit up and some people love to talk about themselves. Most people fall in between, and that is where—this *is* an opinion—the writer's skill lies: building the bridge between what is real and imagined, blending craft and authenticity in an entertaining or affecting way.

There is no fiction in this book. It is of the *non* variety: not, no, none. In some cases, there is the way I remember things, and my feelings about those things. Perhaps those who recognize themselves within those pieces will feel differently about how things happened, but they are true to me.

I think that's why this whole process has been so hard; there's nothing to hide behind. I spent two decades cultivating a voice fit for artistic criticism, snarky alt-weekly writing, irreverent radio, and a sarcastic internet presence. A persona. I couldn't tell you how many times people have said to me, "You're actually nice," with surprise, and it always makes me sad. My public voice— ribald, disparaging, moralistic—is the kind that makes people want to be mean to me in return. I'm not actually like that, not all the way anyway. And now my whole loser life is on display inside these pages, and I can't quip my way out in real time.

Anyway, here's The Fucking Book.

THE ART THAT TURNED A RURAL TEEN INTO A FEMINIST ADULT

YOU GET WHAT YOU SETTLE FOR:
ON *THELMA & LOUISE*

I grew up in the country and I do not recommend it.

Canadians are known worldwide to be polite but that's just because of our proximity to America, which is known for a much different vibe. Compared to the me-first, fuck-'em-all attitude of the average US citizen, our bland and boring approach to life—"Let me get the door for you!"—appears pleasant and non-confrontational.

But get down here to the Maritimes, to Nova Scotia, and you'll discover very quickly that's not true. Go to a small town on the south shore or in the Annapolis Valley and walk into a diner or through a mall—you'll be stared at, the disdain and distrust emanating from the permanent residents like a puritanical fog. They don't know you, so they don't like you.

Rural Nova Scotia is old and white and Christian and that's the way they want it to be forever. Some of my peers have moved to the country, usually with their young families, and they've tried to reframe rural life as something aspirational, quiet and beautiful. You can't fool me. I came from there and I will never go back.

My hometown is called Lantz. It sucked then, as a Podunk dot on the side of RR#2, and it sucks worse now, as a de facto suburb of the Halifax Regional Municipality. (Which technically, bafflingly, starts at Enfield, which is two towns closer to the city and still forty kilometres from downtown Halifax. My dad still lives in the one in between, Elmsdale. I always say I grew up "out by the airport," which, similarly, is nowhere near Halifax proper.)

There wasn't and still isn't a movie theatre. When I was a teenager the closest was Bedford (half an hour away); now it's Truro (same), and you need a car to get to either. My parents worked in the city and didn't want to drive there on the weekends, so we didn't. I didn't see a movie in a theatre until my friends could drive.

My mother loved movies, though. There was a constant pile of plastic VHS boxes at our house. Occasionally there'd be one that stuck—*Dirty Dancing* is one of my favourite films to this day—but mostly she was into shitty action stuff, like *Star Wars*. Jean-Claude Van Damme was a big star then. Stallone. Schwarzenegger. A bunch of garbage. I don't know how I ended up being a bit of a movie snob. All signs pointed in a different direction.

In 1992 I was thirteen and *Thelma & Louise* had finally made it to video. I was just starting to become media literate, moving from the likes of *16* and *Bop* magazines—with their pinups of milquetoast famous boys I would stick to my walls; I liked Chad Allen best, he turned out to be gay (cough)—into the cool-girl wonderland of Jane Pratt and Christina Kelly's *Sassy* and movie publications like *Premiere* and *Entertainment Weekly*. I didn't know much about *Thelma & Louise* except that a woman, Callie Khouri, had written it, and people were very mad about it.

The previous summer, Susan Sarandon and Geena Davis had appeared on the cover of *Time* with small, wry smiles above a headline declaring "Why *Thelma & Louise* Strikes a Nerve," not that I read the actual story back then. Which nerve?! I had no idea.

Though she hadn't seen the film herself, my mother had refused to let me see it, probably because the inciting incident is a sexual assault, so I did what I would do throughout my entire adolescence when a film I wanted to see was deemed controversial at home: I went to a friend's house. (Devious!)

I can still remember sitting on my friend's living room floor in absolute shock.

"THEY DIED?!"

It was unfathomable to me, then, that heroes could die. This was not the Hollywood I knew, where men ruled and when they were wronged they avenged and, despite rather outlandish odds, always won. The hero was forever standing at the end, battered but victorious. In *Thelma & Louise*, the heroes were frozen in their death fall into the Grand Canyon. Ridley Scott shot the whole thing—the convertible dropping down, flipping into the rocks, and exploding—but the movie stops when the car is at its highest point and fades to white, as if hope remained.

It fucking didn't. I was devastated.

When people say a movie changed their life, this is the kind of movie they mean. It moved my cells around. But it didn't make me believe in the power of cinema, or art, or even sisterhood. It made me understand how the odds were stacked against women, even when they deserved justice, even when they were right. Why stay and fight when you knew you would lose? And fight for what, exactly? Bad men and dead dreams? (This may also be where the seeds of my enduring nihilistic streak were planted.) It was sobering and galvanizing.

Somewhere in my grief, I became a feminist.

*

Thelma & Louise begins like a buddy comedy: Louise (Sarandon) is a tough, no-nonsense waitress. Her best friend, Thelma (Davis), is a ditzy housewife with a shitty husband. We meet them on the eve of a girls' weekend away. What shenanigans will they get up to at Louise's boss's cabin?! Stay tuned!

Of course, they never get to the cabin. They stop at a roadhouse—they live in Arkansas, a state which notably practices capital punishment—for a drink at Thelma's urging: "I never get to do stuff like this!" A regular sets his sights on Thelma, gets her drunk, spins her into dizziness on the dance floor, and slips her outside when Louise is in the bathroom. In the parking lot she throws up, but he kisses her anyway.

She doesn't want to kiss, she's married. But his kiss turns to a slap and soon he's bending her over a car, ripping his belt off, pushing her head down and telling her to shut up.

A gun appears in the frame and its barrel comes to rest behind the man's left ear, at the base of his skull. It's held with familiarity and skill by Louise who, we find out later, has been through this herself. Her finger is on the trigger.

As a weeping and bruised Thelma stumbles away out of the man's sweaty hands, Louise—still wielding the gun—gives him a small speech through her clenched jaw: "In the future, when a woman's crying like that, she isn't having any fun!" They turn and start walking away. "Bitch!" he screams. They keep walking. And then: "I should have gone ahead and fucked her."

Now Louise turns around, wild-eyed. "What did you say?" The reply: "I said, 'Suck my cock.'"

This is the part, I believe, that caused the fury. *That's* when Louise shoots him. They're armed. They're leaving. They're no longer in danger. The shooting is not in self-defense.

This sets off a series of crimes that, taken at face value, do not paint a picture to get behind, even if you support the murder of rapists (I do): Thelma robs a store, she and Louise put a police officer in the trunk of his own cruiser at gunpoint, and they (improbably) blow up a giant truck.

Add the context, though: Two women survive something violent and traumatizing; have all their money stolen by Brad Pitt (hence the robbery); are trying to avoid arrest for two crimes (hence the cop); and that truck's driver has been harassing them across the American South (hence the kaboom).

Once they go on the run, their entire existence becomes about merely surviving—ironic, considering the ending.

*

In the wake of its success in the early '90s, *Thelma & Louise* was expected to change things for women—actors, writers, directors, stories—but as Davis lamented in *Vanity Fair* on the film's twenty-fifth anniversary in 2016, "It didn't change shit."

Just five years later that's less true than it used to be, but it's hard to know whether these advancements for women in cinema signify a real change or a brief trend. Writer-director Emerald Fennell won the 2021 Academy Award for Best Original

Screenplay—twenty-nine years after Callie Khouri's win; Diablo Cody is the only woman winner in between—for *Promising Young Woman*, about a woman so hellbent on avenging her best friend's rape and suicide that she puts herself in dangerous company nightly. In her incendiary series *I May Destroy You*, Michaela Coel tries to piece together the events leading up to her sexual assault, resulting in an otherworldly series finale exploring multiple outcomes, including one where she takes violent revenge on her rapist. In David Gordon Green's 2018 reboot of *Halloween* and its 2021 sequel, *Halloween Kills*, three generations of Strode women—Jamie Lee Curtis, Judy Greer, and Andi Matichak—battle their family's tormentor, Michael Myers, together. The early 2020 remake of *The Invisible Man*, marketed as a relentless attack on Elisabeth Moss by her abusive husband who faked his death, is a surprisingly sharp look at emotional abuse and gaslighting (with an incredibly satisfying revengending).

I've lost count of how many times I've seen *Thelma & Louise*. I'll watch it any time (just ask me), and I love seeing people experience it for the first time. I made my own feminist vigilante movie, *Compulsus*, in 2021 and put Thelma's words in my hero Wally's mouth: "Something's crossed over in me." Wally has recently taken to attacking abusive hipster men at night, not because she herself has been abused, but because everyone else she knows has. When pressed by a new crush for her motivations, her only defense is that someone needs to do something and, for no reason in particular—there actually is one; I'm not a misandrist with no purpose—she's decided she's doing it.

The back half of Thelma's line is "...and I can't go back." Because I've lived with Thelma and Louise for thirty years I didn't need Wally to explicitly state this. Because you get what you settle for, and we're not going back.

Now, there has been no worldwide revolution in which everyone is equal and no one hurts anyone and we're all treated with respect and kindness. Admitted/convicted rapists and abusers—Chris Brown, Louis CK, Mike Tyson—are doing just fine. *But.* Assault survivors are no longer sitting in ashamed silence suffering alone with their pain—perpetrators are being called out, and publicly, and paying for their actions in the form of job losses and, one hopes, social exclusion. (This is so-called "cancel culture," which does not exist. Accountability is not cancellation. If you don't want to be "cancelled," don't be a sack of shit. Pretty simple, and easy.)

Even as Planned Parenthood clinics burn, even as US Republicans successfully overturn *Roe v. Wade*, as states implement laws that define late-term abortions after six weeks—repeated, blatant, bad-faith attacks on the rights of those with uteruses, so scared are the straight white men of the space they've had pulled back from them—there's a resistance to this institutional misogyny that I've never witnessed in my lifetime. Perhaps it's because we've lived long enough in the age of the climate change protest, of Black Lives Matter, of supporting trans rights, of anti-gun lobbying, that people have realized the only way to change things is to get out in the streets, fuck shit up, and force an international lens onto the issues. It shouldn't have to be this way—you shouldn't have to know what to do when you get tear-gassed just so you can access medical care—but until things *are* equal, this is the way it is.

There is no more just living with it. There is no more settling. There is no going back.

I HAVEN'T GOT BALL PLAYERS, I'VE GOT GIRLS: ON *A LEAGUE OF THEIR OWN*

Penny Marshall shot a million feet of film for *A League of Their Own*. Her first cut was four hours long. The ultimate two hours and eight minutes—ditch the reunion framework and you'd have something closer to a perfect ninety minutes—is a history lesson; a gold-standard sports movie; an ensemble comedy featuring dozens of women, including Madonna (in her best, most subversive role—fight me); and a rumination on dreams, sisterhood, and gendered societal roles.

No big deal.

First and foremost, *A League of Their Own* is of course about baseball.

We meet Dottie (Geena Davis, a builder of my 1990s feminist film bedrock) and her younger sister Kit (Lori Petty) at a recreational softball game in their rural Oregon town. We see right away that Dottie's the star and Kit's a wild card—she has some talent but she can't harness it, whereas her sister is dismissive bordering on aloof about her own remarkable skills.

(Let my stance be known from the jump: Kit is a baby who is only OK at best and Dottie does her a favour by dropping the ball in their eventual pivotal World Series final, not that Kit—a brat with an inferiority complex—would ever appreciate it. Shut up, Kit.)

Jon Lovitz appears in an all-timer of a brief performance as a scout who recruits them for the All-American Girls Professional Baseball League, which a candy magnate, Mr. Harvey—a stand-in for Mr. Wrigley—has funded to make a buck while all the real baseball players are fighting in World War II. He doesn't want Kit, but he'll take her if she can convince Dottie ("the one who hit the ball") to try out in Chicago.

They both make it onto the Rockford Peaches, of course, but by the movie's climax, Dottie the superstar catcher and Kit the erratic pitcher (and worse hitter) are on opposing teams in the World Series and no longer speaking to one another. As Kit crouches into her batting stance, Dottie calls "time"—a total psyche—and walks out to the mound with a directive for her team's pitcher: "High fastballs. She can't hit 'em, you can't lay off 'em."

Except Kit does hit one of 'em, sending the right-fielder scrambling after her triple. The third-base coach signals for her to stop but she doesn't, barrelling toward home and her waiting sister, whose skill, beauty, and popularity Kit's always considered impediments to her own success.

Now, about the dropping of the ball, which is still somehow a point of debate thirty years later: We see Dottie catch the long throw from the outfield and she's holding the ball, glove out, as Kit's coming into home. Then Kit runs over Dottie at the plate. As she falls, Dottie's got the glove against herself—Marshall shows us three different angles of the impact, in slow motion— but the ball is in her right hand. When she hits the ground hard, flat on her back, her bare right hand bounces off the dirt and the ball rolls out of it.

It may surprise you to learn I was a catcher for many years, so I actually know about this (and only this; sports-wise, I am a traitor to my people). First of all, the ball is thrown to Dottie with plenty of time to tag Kit out. The play is certainly time-sensitive, but it's not a race of any kind. Second, a catcher of Dottie's calibre is not going to stand there, with that amount of time, with the baseball in her bare hand. It's going in the glove, then that glove is going against the body.

It was a total fucking dive. Indisputably. (Marshall, who died in 2018, says as much on the fifteenth-anniversary DVD commentary. But also, it's obvious.)

Nothing leading up to that moment indicates anything like this is going to happen. Dottie fully tells the pitcher how to defeat Kit. She glares at her as she passes, staring daggers into the back of her sister's head. She wants to take her out. But then she doesn't. Instead, she hands Kit her future, and Kit doesn't even see it happen. She thinks—and there is no evidence she ever reconsiders the events of that day—not that her sister fucked up, but that she, Kit, finally bested Dottie. It's simply not true, but the grace of Dottie is that she lets Kit believe it.

This is a movie absolutely filled with grace (gracefully and grandly), not just in the athletics but in the characterizations of women of the era and issues of the time—save, notably, homosexuality; Rosie O'Donnell, publicly closeted during filming, has since said she was playing Doris gay.

There is Dottie, tall and glamourous even in her farmer's clothes, and Kit, small and scrappy, living their dusty, go-nowhere life on the dairy farm. Dottie has just married Bob (Bill Pullman), the assistant manager at the dairy ("He's gonna be manager someday, he's real smart"), and she wants to stay there forever with him and start a family. Kit hates the idea and desperately wants out, but she does not want a man to rescue her. Both choices are valid—no one in the movie, especially Tom Hanks as Peaches coach Jimmy Dugan, can understand why someone as good as Dottie does not want to play, but she doesn't. To her, it's just a game. Real life is on the farm with Bob. For Kit, it's in the city with some teammates and a job she actually cares about.

There is Mae Mordabito (Madonna), who's cleverly riffing on Madonna's real-life image from the time—her kinky/*I'm Breathless* era. Her nickname is literally All The Way Mae yet she gets a speech, when the war ends and the league is about to be shuttered, about how she's found her self-worth in baseball and she's not about to go back to dancing for men.

There is Evelyn (Bitty Schram), forced to bring her shitty kid on the road because her husband is "too busy looking at the want ads." She's the catalyst for Hanks's famous "There's no crying in baseball" scene—and as with all famous lines, the context has been lost to time (see also "Let them eat cake" and "Everything's coming up Milhouse"). Dugan rips into Evelyn after she makes a bad throw, and when she starts crying he goes in on her even harder, telling her a famous coach of his once called him a "talking pile of pig shit" in front of his parents, and did he cry? No!

The point of this scene comes later, after Jimmy—a falldown drunk who believes this favour of a job is beneath him—is sober and redeemed. Evelyn repeats the mistake that caused the outburst, and this time when he confronts her about it, he does so calmly and instructively, with great and hilarious restraint, so she takes the note and feels good about herself afterwards. As opposed to the other way.

There is Betty Spaghetti, played by Marshall's daughter Tracy Reiner, who talks about her husband so much that it really shouldn't surprise you when he dies overseas, but it does because we're supposed to think it's Bob who was killed. She is with her teammates in the dressing room when she receives the worst news of her life, and they instinctively surround her in comfort.

There is Marla Hooch (Megan Cavanagh), initially rejected by Lovitz's scout because even though she's a monster hitter she's not attractive enough. Kit: "You mean you ain't takin' her cause she ain't pretty?" Off the scout's affirmation, in unison, she and Dottie drop their suitcases in a feminist protest, and don't pick them up again until he agrees to let Marla try out. (In a less progressive plot point, a nerdy man falls in love with Marla, which is played for yuks, then she marries him and...quits the team? Marla's character was actually pregnant, which was in the original cut, but clearly some things had to go.)

There are smaller era-specific grace notes threaded throughout, like when Helen (Anne Ramsay) recognizes that Shirley (Ann Cusack) can't read and thus doesn't know whether she made the team (she did); or when a stray ball is thrown back to the pitcher from the sidelines by an African American woman, banned from playing in the league.

*

A League of Their Own boasted a pile of hitmakers circa 1992. Marshall's recent directorial outings, *Big* and *Awakenings*, were both successes. The lead cast was Davis, fresh off an Academy Award nomination and cultural juggernaut in *Thelma & Louise*; Hanks, a thriving comedian about to pivot to Serious Actor; and Madonna, area superstar.

It was released ahead of the lucrative fourth of July weekend in the United States, beginning of tentpole season, a perfect summer movie: Playing the most American of sports, in support of historically successful American war efforts, with Mr. America Tom Hanks making it okay for men to want to see it, too. In those days blockbuster territory was $100 million gross, *total*—a Marvel movie making that on *opening weekend* is now considered a failure—and the team pulled in $132 million worldwide.

It's considered a bona fide sports movie up there with *Field of Dreams* and *Rocky*, as opposed to a "chick flick," although I can't think of any men of my acquaintance who have expressed fervent love for it. It was written by Lowell Ganz and Babaloo Mandel—Marshall said no female screenwriter of the time wanted the job—yet its understanding of the push and pull of sisterhood, the real and emotional kinds, is nuanced and insightful. Even if, say, Kit whips a glove at Doris's head or throws a ball through a window in Dottie's general direction— please just *shut up*, Kit, and wait for therapy to be invented— those outsized action moments pale in comparison to her asking her sister, in a brief and heartbreaking moment of vulnerability, "Why'd ya have to be so good?" Or Mae teaching Shirley how to read using an erotic novel. Or Doris admitting she's dating a loser because none of the other boys were interested in her. Or Evelyn with her ukulele, writing the league's theme song on the bus: "It's about us."

The movie ends in present day, the 1990s, as an AAGPBL exhibit opens at the National Baseball Hall of Fame in Cooperstown, New York. A couple of the Peaches have died or their husbands have (still, nobody's gay), and so has Jimmy Dugan, but mostly they're aged versions of the people we met in the main timeline, older and happy.

Kit walks in with many ginger grandchildren and has a joyful reunion with Dottie. It's not explicitly stated, but it seems like it's been a long time since they've seen each other. They're friendly, but clearly not close. Maybe the World Series split them forever; maybe life just pushed them apart, as it does. Their hug is happy, and genuine.

The movie ends with the old gals playing a game as Madonna performs "This Used to Be My Playground," a ballad written for the film during her *Erotica* sessions. (For doubtlessly ridiculous record company reasons, it was not on the film's actual sound-track compilation CD and/or cassette.)

It's a boldly sentimental note for a movie that insists there's no crying in baseball: its minor, string-laden melody drifts in gentle contrast against the fun and sassy low-stakes match we're watching, which has senior citizens making sweet plays and kicking dirt on the umpire's shoes in protest of a call. It throws back to the original rec-league game in which we saw Dottie and Kit playing back in the first act, before they have a foot race back to the farm, a bit of levity and escape from their humdrum lives.

The difference, now that we're at the end of the movie, is we know all that was to come for them, what they gave up to get it, and everything they earned. "'Don't hold onto the past,'" Madonna sings. "Well, that's too much to ask."

ME AND A GUN AND A MAN ON MY BACK: TORI AMOS, FROM *LITTLE EARTHQUAKES* TO *FROM THE CHOIRGIRL HOTEL*

T ori Amos came to me the way everything did growing up in the country: by total accident.

It was a Friday night in the winter of 1996, and I was doing what all cool fifteen-year-olds of the time were doing: Watching *Primetime Live with Diane Sawyer*.

It was the eve of the album *Boys for Pele* and Tori was doing the media rounds. (This is also when I learned about promotional cycles, which within five years would be a large part of my professional life.) Though she is from the American South, she spoke in an accent of her own making, with quiet authority, about how she didn't want to play "dead guys' music" and did want to redefine the piano and composition for it in a contemporary way. She had red hair, big lips, and fucked-up teeth—I thought she was the strangest, most alluring woman I'd ever seen.

The piece was a typical for-the-boomers overview of her life, but it was all new to me then: Her preacher father, her life as a child prodigy, her stint playing in gay bars in DC, her failed LA glam career. I watched with momentary interest, but the voice-over took a dark turn at the halfway point: *Little Earthquakes*'s "centrepiece was a haunting anthem called 'Me and a Gun,' which spoke to many women. Tori Amos sang about the time she was raped."

The voice- over was followed by a live clip of Tori singing, "Me and a gun / and a man on my back," a cappella as it is on the record, to a dead silent room.

Then came the quote that locked me in forever. "I saw *Thelma & Louise*," Tori said, "and it brought up things even I didn't understand. And I think there's some things that, um, I don't wanna remember."

Did you go to the police or anything? Tori closed her eyes, shook her head. "No, no." She looked up, like she might cry. A cut, and the angle changed. "It's not that simple. Sometimes you're in a situation where if you come forth, you're nailed. The law isn't, ah, supportive of violent situations for women. Come on, I was a nightclub singer. I dressed sexy. Look—let's not kid each other. My case was closed before I began."

Did you think it was your fault? "Yeah. I did. Violence is such a strange experience. If you feel that kind of hate from another person. It's like, it gets into your cells. It gets into every part of your being. And so I've been committing myself to becoming a phoenix out of the ashes for myself."

Later in the piece she said, "My commitment is to crossing over that river, the river of victimhood. But you have to be in that river, you will be in that river, if you've been violated. I'm really at a place where I believe you can heal. You can heal, and yet not forget, and it's a new way of thinking."

I was stunned. It was the first time I'd heard someone talk so openly about rape, which was still a new concept to me even in a post–*Thelma & Louise* world. This was before I fell asleep babysitting and woke up to the rape scene in *The Accused* (more on Jodie Foster later).

The next night Tori was on *Saturday Night Live* (promo!). The music *Primetime Live* had played was largely solo piano stuff, so as not to scare its key demographic, and other than "Me and a Gun" I'd barely noticed it. For her first *SNL* segment she played "Caught A Lite Sneeze," a thunderously weird, glorious song that's rumoured to be about a botched romance with Trent Reznor (note the reference to a "pretty hate machine," also the title of Nine Inch Nails's debut record). The *Pele* era was when Amos introduced her now-standard stage setup, planted between a Bösendorfer piano and a harpsichord. She stood in the middle of those instruments, dressed down in a scoop-neck T-shirt and tight skirt, writhing and ripping through the complicated melody like it was nothing, singing directly into the camera through her bright red hair.

An ethereal woman theatrically pounded giant drums in the back, and eight members of a boys' choir up way past their bedtimes sang the chorus's high countermelody (performed on the record by Tori herself). Just as I'd never seen a woman who looked like her, before that moment I'd never heard a voice like hers. It was one thing to hear her speak with compelling intellect about sexual assault and being a child phenom, but it was quite another to see her perform the music itself. It was thrilling, electrifying, inspiring.

Her second song for the show was a complete 180 from "Caught A Lite Sneeze," in both presentation and vibe: A solo performance of the gentle, devastated post-breakup

24

resignation called "Hey Jupiter," which has been a mainstay of my post-everything wallow in the twenty-five years since. (I quoted it in my high school yearbook.)

*

I don't remember much about music before this time. My parents had a couple crates of uncared-for vinyl out of the '70s and '80s, lots of Air Supply and Springsteen and whatnot, certainly not the handed-down music education I hear so many artists talk about. I was a preteen in the pop heyday of Tiffany and Debbie Gibson, and I loved them both—even though I felt Debbie was more of An Artist because she wrote her own songs and Tiffany didn't. I distinctly remember a grade 6 discussion about the new sound and look of New Kids on the Block's *Step by Step*. But what came between NKOTB and Tori, I couldn't tell you.

As Tori's life was changed by *Thelma & Louise*, her music would come to have as much impact on my life as that film. I bought *Boys For Pele* on CD at a Records on Wheels in Bedford (an absolutely outlandish sentence in modern times). The album is about Tori's breakup with Eric Rosse, who she was with for seven years; he produced her 1992's breakthrough *Little Earthquakes* and 1994's *Under the Pink*. Here Tori produced herself for the first time, and it's likely one of the reasons *Boys For Pele* is so sprawling—at eighteen tracks and seventy minutes, it was the longest album I'd ever heard. (As if I would listen to *Mellon Collie and the Infinite Sadness*.)

It's an album full of deep loss, flailing, anger, melancholy, and darkness. When she's not dissecting relationships, she's singing murder ballads about shooting men and hiding out. For every melodically pleasing piano ballad à la "Father Lucifer" or "Doughnut Song," there's a downright ugly counterpoint in the form of "Professional Widow" (Courtney Love, supposedly) or "Blood Roses," their sharp harpsichord notes cutting through growling, fuck-everything rage like a horror-movie soundtrack. It's never sweet or cowering, but it contains many moments of great delicacy and tenderness, as when she sings about a beautiful but ruinous man on "Putting the Damage On." He wrecked your life, but *look at him.*

Little Earthquakes (1992) had reintroduced Tori Amos as a recovered hair-band artist, authentic now, just a girl and her piano. *Under the Pink* expanded a bit from its predecessor, with its gentle ruminations on masturbation ("Icicle") and emotional abuse ("Bells for Her") counterbalanced by the weird guitars of "Space Dog," the defiantly provocative "God," and her one true hit, "Cornflake Girl." *Boys For Pele* took all the outsized, experimental moments from those records—the grunge flare-ups and guttural vocals of "Pretty Good Year," "Precious Things," and "Waitress," the baroque show tuneliness of "Wrong Band," "Happy Phantom," and "Leather," and the Steinman-esque epicness of the two closers, "Little Earthquakes" and "Yes, Anastasia" (as in Romanov!)—and made them the root of its sound.

Pele played then as it does now: like a fever dream, a Broadway show, an art film. A one-of-a-kind experience with no precedent (lazy Kate Bush comparisons are sometimes apt, but not for this record), and the artist has lived in its long shadow for the decades since. (Supposedly she doesn't like to play its songs at all.) It is, in my view, her masterwork.

*

The Tori who shows up on *From* the *Choirgirl Hotel* in 1998, two years later, is markedly different from the one who thrashed her way through *Pele*. Much was made at the time of her dip into electronica, an era-dominant genre, but outside of some drum programming it's really only two songs—the full-on club banger "Raspberry Swirl" (era star Armand Van Helden remixed it later) and the brash and whiplash-inducing "Hotel."

In between records Tori had fallen in love with one of *Pele*'s engineers, Mark Hawley; they married and subsequently suffered two miscarriages, which *Choirgirl* explores in uncommon, intimate detail. She digs into the guilt, the grief, and the gut-wrenching disappointment of loss in slow, dramatic songs like "Spark" and "Playboy Mommy."

That summer I was between my first and second years of university and part of a youth theatre group that wrote and staged its own one-act plays. (That's right, I've always been cool.) The previous year I'd made a two-hander called *Orange Clouds*, an overwrought, overdramatic fifteen minutes only a teen could write, setting the final speech against "Silent All These Years." Never one to mess with success, such as it ever has been, I repeated the format and used *From the Choirgirl Hotel* as my muse for that year's play, *Change Like Sugar Cane*. (The title is taken from a line from "Northern Lad.")

This is the kind of fervent drama Tori inspires in grown people, not just adolescents who don't know any better, and it's why you either love her or you have no time for her deal. The casual Tori Amos fan does not exist. She once famously said, and you can find it on a meme, "I know I'm an acquired taste. I'm anchovies."

*

In 2001 Tori was about to set out in support of her covers record, *Strange Little Girls*, when 9/11 happened. On the day of its release—September 18—she appeared as David Letterman's first musical guest in this new world, in a city broken and grieving, and performed Tom Waits's "Time," with its simple and apt refrain that it's time that we love.

Letterman, never one to show much emotion, walked over to her clapping and pulled her into a hug, in tears.

Tori visited every US state on that tour, and thirteen months later—standard record cycles are two years—released what, were I not Canadian, I would consider her masterwork over *Pele*: *Scarlet's Walk*, a cinematic concept album that begins in California with "Amber Waves" (named for the porn star played by Julianne Moore in *Boogie Nights*) and through its heroine, Scarlet, wanders the nation across eighteen songs, stopping off in major cities and passing through endless rural stretches.

The seven-minute twelfth track, "I Can't See New York," puts Scarlet on a plane on 9/11—it reads callously, but empathy is one of Tori's greatest strengths as an artist; she was also in New York City on the day—while managing to move between the first and third person, using this and every song on the record to interrogate the very idea of "America." It begins on the flight and ends somewhere on the ground, in the metaphorical rubble of the War on Terror.

The very land the United States was built on, and the question of who owns it or any land, comes up in sundry ways, most significantly in the forty-four-second a capella "Wampum Prayer," in honour of Tori's Cherokee grandfather, that observes bloodstains and churches in tandem on the land (earlier, on "A Sorta Fairytale," she notes that Americans are "imposters" in their country). And on "Sweet Sangria," Scarlet grapples with border police in Texas, wondering about "the innocents" on both sides.

One of her specialties is threading micro into macro, so even as she frames the United States with a wide lens, she also moves in close for devastating moments of intimacy. "Taxi Ride" is part homage to her friend Kevyn Aucoin, the late makeup artist: "Just another dead fag to you / just another light missing / on a long taxi ride." On the album's closer, "Gold Dust," Scarlet gives birth, new life emerging from loss and chaos, hope rising out of the smoking wreckage of America.

*

Tori Amos has released nine albums and made a musical, *The Light Princess*, since *Scarlet's Walk*. Results vary—as with any career artist, the buzz burns off but the faithful remain—and there are tracks on all of them that rival anything on these five records. (One of my favourites, surprisingly to me, is "Our New Year" from *Midwinter Graces*, her 2009 Christmas album.) But together they comprise a formidable, barely rivalled—name me someone!—decade of work, the indisputable best stretch of her career.

She's nearly sixty now, and I am a decade past the age at which Tori Amos reinvented herself—or rather, started living authentically—and started over. I'm older than she was when she made all five of these albums, older than she was when she was assaulted, and ended a major relationship, and got married, and miscarried, and witnessed from the ground one of the worst terrorist attacks in a nation's history and its effects on that nation.

The music she made in the wake of those times, even if it's not at the top of my daily playlist currently, remains as important to me as it was when I first heard it, when I held it close and it carried me.

Often we outgrow the artists we love, because they don't change with us, and that's not their fault—some music just serves a certain time in our life. It's said that the age at which you enter the music industry is the age you're frozen at forever—it certainly explains The Rolling Stones and Red Hot Chili Peppers—but Tori, as many women have had to, belies that adage. She doesn't chase trends or sound like she's from a certain era anymore. Her music has grown and evolved with her, maintaining the same shrewd and observant eye, peerless melodic composition, and hot piano skills. If you need it now, it's there for you, wherever and however you are.

THE 1990S FILMS OF JODIE FOSTER

The same way I don't have memories of the music I liked between grades 6 and 11, I don't remember who my favourite actor was before Jodie Foster.

I arrived at her work in a rather horrific way when I was fifteen: One Saturday night I was babysitting and the parents were late as usual, and I dozed off on the couch. I woke up to the rape scene in *The Accused*.

What that scene was even doing on television is a fair question of its own—I remember specifically that it was a west coast affiliate, so this was airing around 8:00 P.M. in Vancouver or wherever—but what it was doing in a movie at all is another. (I'm not going to describe it.)

In *The Accused*, which came out in 1988 and was written by a man and directed by another man, Foster plays Sarah Tobias, who is gang-raped in a bar on top of a pinball machine. Not only is the act watched by dozens of people, some of those people cheer it on like they're at a football game. On the night of the attack Sarah was wearing a short skirt, had taken recreational drugs, and most importantly was an alcoholic with a drug-dealer boyfriend.

The movie is about the aftermath and the trial, the way the details of a survivor's life are used against them to demonstrate that obviously their own choices led to some man—men— assaulting them. You've heard this a million times. I rolled my eyes just typing it. But in 1988 (and in whatever year you're reading this, let's be honest), rape trials were pitched this way: not "What made the man assault the person?" but "What did the person do to deserve it?"

The filmmaker in me understands that to hang a story on an assault and not show the assault is to undercut your own narrative. Nowadays, in the age of intimacy coordinators and survivor-centred works like *I May Destroy You*, the rape may have been filmed differently than director Jonathan Kaplan staged it, in all its plain, brutal, public violence. In the late 1980s, however, Foster had to live through it. "She wasn't penetrated, but the sequence was 90 percent real," Kaplan told Rachel Abramowitz in *Premiere* in 1995. "She had to do it over and over again."

In that suburban East Hants living room the following decade, as Sarah Tobias fled the bar weeping, the parents of the kids I was babysitting returned. I snapped the TV off in shame, like they'd caught me watching porn. The dad drove me home and I sat stunned in the passenger seat, saying nothing about what I'd just seen, then I ran into my own basement and threw the movie back on.

It was now the very end, when the verdict comes down. Present-day Sarah Tobias gets sober, obtains a truly terrible haircut, and wins her case.

I've never seen the whole movie and I don't want to. But I was instantly intrigued by Foster's sharp face, warm eyes, and fierce intellect. I was tangentially aware of her because I was religiously reading movie magazines by that point and she was often on the cover of them. I knew that in a sea of starlets and romantic comedy leads—your Julia Robertses, your Meg Ryans—she was the serious, smart one. I knew she had quit Hollywood to go to Yale (*The Accused* was her comeback, and she won her first Academy Award for it). I knew she was curiously single. But I wasn't overly familiar with her work.

I'd seen *Maverick* because in the 1990s when Mel Gibson made a movie you watched it, even if it was a frothy Western. (It's basically the only time Foster has been funny.) And the drama/romance *Sommersby* (bad) because my mom was into Richard Gere. And *Nell* because it was a cultural punchline (ta-ae in the wind and all that).

I had missed the juggernaut that was *The Silence of the Lambs* because I thought it was a horror movie and I hated those. (It's not not a horror movie, but it's also one of the best films ever made.) So I started there and worked my way around, back to weird '70s things like the child gangster musical *Bugsy Malone* and Disney's *Candleshoe*; caught up with her directorial debut, *Little Man Tate*, about a child genius; tracked down a pair of tough gems from 1980: *Foxes*, Adrian Lyne's debut about a teen foursome, and *Carny*, in which Foster is caught in an unfortunate love triangle with Robbie Robertson and Gary Busey. (Keep in mind these were nascent DVD and internet times, so when I say "tracked down" I don't mean through a streaming service or torrent, I mean I walked to the weird video store or bought the VHS on eBay and paid triple the price of the tape in shipping to Canada from the midwestern United States.)

Foster has been working since she was three years old and has no formal training. (At Yale, with its famous acting program, she studied literature.) She literally grew up on sets, on 1970s sitcoms and in Disney movies. She famously graduated to adult roles when she was thirteen and co-starred with Robert De Niro in *Taxi Driver*, playing a sex worker. This is the role that inspired a man to attempt to assassinate Ronald Reagan in 1981, to impress her.

After winning her Oscar for *The Accused*—a role the studio and producers didn't even want her for; Kaplan had to sneak her the sides for her self-tape—Foster accrued the clout to really do what she wanted. That included directing *Little Man Tate*, in which she cast herself as the single mother of a preternaturally gifted son, art imitating life: though she was the youngest of four children, not an only child, Foster grew up with a single mother and started paying the bills when she was ten.

It included starring in *The Silence of the Lambs* and winning her second Oscar—over both Geena Davis and Susan Sarandon for *Thelma & Louise*, a movie she nearly starred in alongside Michelle Pfeiffer (would still watch)—and starting her own production company. She made *Nell*, a misunderstood drama about a wild child–type of woman tripped over by some scientists. She made guest voice appearances on the shows of the day, *The X-Files* and *Frasier*. She directed a second film, *Home for the Holidays* (1995), a Thanksgiving family dramedy starring Holly Hunter and Robert Downey Jr. She was wildly mismatched with Matthew McConaughey for the 1997 Carl Sagan adaptation *Contact*, a thoughtful and well-made daddy issues story (in space). And she stepped in, very pregnant, for an injured Nicole

Kidman in 2002's *Panic Room,* a $200 million-grossing David Fincher action drama about a woman trying to save her daughter from burglars on the first night in their new house.

In this current age where the franchise is the star—ask me about how I hate it!—it's hard to imagine how A-list actors ruled then. Now someone will clamour to be thirteenth billed in a Marvel movie, but in the 1980s and especially the 1990s, movies lived and died by who was in them.

Foster, at the height of her powers from 1988 to 2002, picked roles the way her male peers did: She would be the lone wolf at the centre, with the whole movie pitched in service to her. Occasionally there would be a love interest—more on this very soon—but generally not, because she didn't like to appear vulnerable. As Clarice Starling or Ellie Arroway or Meg Altman, she would be on some sort of quest. She would use intelligence and perseverance to win. And she always did. Movie-star shit. (Tom Cruise and Will Smith still do this.)

But there was another reason Foster did not play romantic leads, and it wasn't just because she thought they were frivolous, although she surely did. It took me not long to realize it's also the reason she became my favourite actor and why I felt compelled to see everything she'd ever done: She was a closeted lesbian.

Back then it was called the "glass" closet—everyone knew, but no one said anything. "Everyone" meant Hollywood people, not the average American filmgoer, who didn't care much about Foster's personal life anyway because her movies were small and dramatic and she literally was not Julia Roberts, the only lady movie star we cared about in the '90s. But in addition to my film magazines I also read the *National Enquirer,* and from it I learned that Foster was in a long-term relationship with a woman named Cydney Bernard, a film producer, with whom she had two children.

They'd broken up, apparently amicably, after two decades together and not long before Foster was awarded the Cecil B. DeMille Award for lifetime achievement at the Golden Globes in 2013. Foster's speech starts out riffing, as she exclaims "I'm fifty!" à la Molly Shannon while pumping her toned arms, followed by a few jokes and gratitude for her co-stars and crew. Then she gets uncharacteristically nervous, her voice shaking, and says, "While I'm here being all confessional, I guess I just have a sudden urge to say something I've never, um, really been able to air in public, so, declaration that I'm maybe a little nervous about but not quite as nervous as my publicist right now... Loud and proud, right?" Then she leans into the mic. "I am... single."

The crowd laughs, uneasily. Cut to her boys in tuxes, also laughing.

"I hope you won't be disappointed that this isn't a big coming-out speech tonight, because I already did my coming out about a thousand years ago back in the Stone Age."

She goes on to say that she told the people who were close to her—"who actually knew me"—and she isn't going to have a press conference ("a fragrance and a reality TV show") about it. And then touts the value of privacy. Thanks her team and Mel Gibson. And then Bernard, very kindly—"my heroic co-parent, my ex-partner in love but righteous soul sister in life, my confessor, ski buddy, consigliere, most beloved BFF of twenty years"—and then, tearing up, her dying mother.

Not once does she say lesbian, or queer.

As someone who had been waiting for this speech for twenty years I thought Foster seemed scared, but then again she is one of our best actors. Maybe she was off-script, maybe she was pushing herself to do it and couldn't, we'll never know. I do know the gold-star gays on Twitter were mad about it, calling her cowardly; many of them had likely not even been alive long enough to know about the Reagan situation. Though she made the point to underline that she'd been in the public eye for forty-seven years and there were things she kept to herself, they saw someone still in the ostensible closet as backwards and out of touch.

"Was Jodie Foster's 'Coming Out' a Step Backward for Gays and Lesbians?" sniffed *The New York Times*—note mocking quotation use around "coming out." But then, a curveball: The column itself was supportive. "It's the life-changing blink of an eye in which we shed our skins and ask to be known—and loved—for who we are," wrote Steven Petrow. "And that's exactly what she said: 'I want to be seen, to be understood deeply and to be not so very lonely.' Isn't that one of the most compelling reasons to leave the closet? Isn't that what we all want in the end?"

In 2021 Foster was a surprise Golden Globe winner for Best Supporting Actress in *The Mauritanian*. She'd said in that infamous DeMille speech that she might never be on that stage to accept an award again, and in a way she was right—it was Covid times, so she was at home accepting over Zoom in fancy pyjamas. The other big difference? Seated next to her was her wife, actor Alexandra Hedison. When Foster's name was announced, they kissed, smooshing their dog between them.

This is how the world has changed now—someone who'd seemingly decided to stay in the closet forever, who'd very publicly doubled down on it seven years previous, was here in her late fifties just going for it. (It certainly helps to have a nest egg from the A-list acting career you abandoned/aged out of to fall back on if it backfired. I wish.) A reliably classy and well-put-together awards show attendee historically, Foster never looked better or more relaxed. And this performance was a rare one— she's mostly directing television these days.

But in the 1990s, Jodie Foster forged a singular kind of female movie star that we only see occasionally now in a Jessica Chastain or a Jennifer Lawrence (and even they are part of comic-book franchises). Steely, serious, prestige acting. Intelligence over everything. Legacy and longevity. And constant evolution.

IT'S NOT FAIR TO DENY ME: ALANIS MORISSETTE, *JAGGED LITTLE PILL* (ON MUSIC SNOBBERY)

Music snobbery is for men and squares. "Guilty pleasures" are just regular things jerks make you feel bad about liking. Another essay for another time would be how "guilty pleasure" needs to be reframed to mean music you still listen to even though it's made by a monster, like Phil Spector or R. Kelly. You should feel guilty about that.

There's a difference between being a fucking snob, just some humourless cunt who doesn't even like music—a good friend of mine once dated a guy who only listened to Pavement, imagine—and having standards. If you are a fan of the go-to punching bag in this conversation, Nickelback, that's your business. But based on the standards of lyrical quality, melody, guitar tone, and hair product, you are wrong. That's not me being a snob, it's just common sense. A lot of people love The National— its tastefully composed, monotone indie-dad-rock is not for me—but I understand based on the same standards applied to Nickelback that The National is objectively good, even if I also think it's what the colour beige would sound like if it started a band.

U2 has been one of the biggest bands in the world as long as I've been alive and in my opinion they have one good song ("With Or Without You"). But Bono is a great, if unexciting, singer! They are political! They have soaring guitar lines! They know how to work a stadium! It does not affect me in any way if you like U2. I often say this about movies: I don't like it, but I understand why someone would.

I learned this distinction the hard way in 1995. Alanis Morissette's "You Oughta Know" and its desert-hot video dropped out of the sky—via Madonna's new imprint Maverick Records—and blew a hole in music as we knew it, asking very plainly: "Would she go down on you in a theatre?"

I was in grade 10 and they always blanked out "down on you" (and of course the killer "fuck" denouement) on the radio and I never knew what that line was supposed to be, and then when I found out I could only kind of guess what it meant. Shoutout to Hants East Rural High's non-existent sexual education program!

But this woman, Alanis, was fucking angry in a way we had not seen women be in pop music. When I say "pop" here I expressly mean "popular," because *Jagged Little Pill*—which Alanis created in her early twenties with producer Glen Ballard—is a pure 1990s rock artifact: clearly influenced by the already waning grunge era, featuring bass by Flea even, all minor notes and discord. And we'd seen the kind of rage Alanis was emanating coming out of Olympia, Washington, with the riot grrrls and of course Courtney Love, but Bikini Kill never sold 30 million records.

I had a problem with "Alanis Morissette," and it was this: She was the former Canadian pop star Alanis, and she'd re-emerged down in America as a fully formed rock goddess, and that made me angry. She'd had a whole-ass career as budget Tiffany, wearing scrunchies and doing choreography, and she thought she could throw on a man's button-down and not wear makeup and we'd all just forget?!

Like, her biggest pre-grunge hit was "Too Hot" and it rhymed "never too old" with "you gotta go for gold." Like!

Because of this I was fervently anti–Miss Suddenly Has A Last Name, rejecting *JLP* for the bulk of its meteoric 1995, until my sister asked me for it for Christmas.

This is something indisputable about the streaming era: it's nearly impossible to learn whole records, let alone give them a chance to grow on you. When you came of age somewhere with garbage commercial radio (hi), no access to a music retailer, and MuchMusic wasn't available through your cable provider until 1997, there were scant places to hear new and popular music. You bought CDs and you listened to them constantly because there was literally nothing else. And—outside of Columbia House's ten-for-a-penny membership deal—they were expensive as fuck, starting at $20. So you got a new record every couple months. It sounds outlandish now, but this was my youth!

So my sister listened to *JLP* constantly, and by this point, eight or nine months on, it was an unstoppable hitmaker—"You Oughta Know," "Ironic," "You Learn," "Head Over Feet"—and therefore inescapable. The record wore me down (reluctantly!) with its wise and incisive lyrics, its incredible voicings, and its uncorking of female rage and desire, two things that were very new to me.

Jagged Little Pill questioned the patriarchy, the Catholic church, the music industry—all systems built by men to oppress and abuse marginalized people. And what I eventually figured out, once I fell off my high horse, was that Alanis could speak to all of this exactly because she'd been a teen pop star. She'd tried to flee that life, ending up on the proverbial couch in Los Angeles with all the other broken dreamers, and from that despair came the best art of her career.

A key facet of music snobbery is a great distrust of ambition. Trying isn't cool. To want success via art is to be vacuous and misguided. But the absolute truth is nobody, in any art form, becomes famous on a lark—from The Ramones to The Strokes to Nirvana to The Weeknd, this has been proven over and over again. No matter the laissez-faire "whatever, man" attitude portrayed in their marketing—key word!—one has to be psychotically ambitious to make it. Nobody moves to Los Angeles or New York—or Vancouver or Toronto, the dollar-store versions of those cities—to make a modest living doing art. Anyone who's ever hit it big practiced a tonne, worked many a room, and leveraged every connection they had.

Fame is never an accident.

To hate something because it's popular, or because its roots are in something you personally find distasteful—bubblegum dance music, say!—is an absolute waste of time. Everyone you listen to, no matter how they come off, has a tiny hope for mass success, for the breakthrough that changes their life and makes music their job.

This conversation is about authenticity. We consider songwriters with addictions more authentic because they've had trouble, they've lived a life most of us will never see. We consider folk music the realest of genres because, as the saying goes, it's a guy and a guitar, no machines or pretense to hide behind. And we consider men to be the arbiters of the artistic human experience even though men have consistently, single-handedly, more than any other demographic in the history of existence, made the human experience worse. We consider the truest genre to be either punk—because it's anti-authority with bad gear and limited skill, because it's not about skill—or hip hop—because it's street poetry, deeply entrenched misogyny be damned. It's not about the delivery, it's about the message.

So how fucking dare, says you and said I back in the '90s, this young woman, barely out of her teens, reappear wielding a distorted guitar and callouts of powerful men? This former Canadian pop star? Not on my watch!

Cut to 2022 and Alanis is a full-on earth mother, the kind of rich California hippie type she probably hated when she was writing *Jagged Little Pill*. This happens to everyone—you get older, you get more money, you become more conservative and way less cool. This happened to almost every scraggly dude who ever made punk blow up. When they interview Debbie Harry in documentaries about 1970s New York, she is always sitting in a lavishly decorated apartment talking about how she had no heat then.

But nothing after—or before—those years can temper or take away from what Alanis accomplished through the back half of the '90s. She broke through a barrier for women in pop music—the monstrous success of Sarah McLachlan's Lilith Fair would not have been possible just a couple years after "You

Oughta Know" dropped, because Alanis challenged and changed the idea that no one wanted to see women on festival stages.

Jagged Little Pill is now a hit Broadway show, a so-called jukebox musical (although does it count when all the songs are by one artist?) with a book by another zeitgeist-catching woman people sure have opinions on, Diablo Cody. Surely the recovering Canadian poplet Alanis never dreamed of that twenty-five years ago when she was squatting at Glen Ballard's house.

The Broadway musical is one of the most artificial, manipulative artistic tools on the planet, reverse-engineered to build in tear-jerking moments (*JLP* apparently has one number that brings the audience to its feet every show). On a stage that big, with that many people involved, intimate nuance is not the goal. (I love Broadway musicals, by the way.)

But its roots are in real life, in real events, in recovery and rebirth and rage. So if *Jagged Little Pill*, the musical, is as authentic as *Jagged Little Pill*, the album, then logic would follow, TARA, that Alanis the pop kid is as authentic as Alanis Morissette, adult rock star.

Being a snob is no accident either. But what's the point?

I'M IN. I AM ALL IN: THE VERBOSE, INSPIRATIONAL, AND CONFLICTING WORK OF AMY SHERMAN-PALLADINO

For the whole of my twenties I felt my way through pretension before I realized that it was a racket. Every person in their twenties goes through this, and it is painful and then it is freeing when you come out on the other side, squinting against the sun, wondering what your problem was. But I, with my altweekly bona fides, would dismiss things, like certain bands or certain women or certain activities, on sight. No research or experience or independent thought, just "Fuck you to this thing!"

One of those things was *Gilmore Girls*, which my little sister, a new teenager deeply entrenched in the target demo at the time (2001ish), loved. It was about a mother and daughter who were [checks notes] best friends. Okay? My relationship with my mother was already drifting badly—I stopped speaking to her on my twenty-fifth birthday, in 2004, midway through *Gilmore*'s run—so I was not, to say the least, interested in this fantasy show on The WB of all networks. And it had "girls" in the title, which to me meant it was "girly," a concept I have fought against my whole life.

I was visiting my dad one summer weekend and alone in the house. For whatever reason, the pilot of *Gilmore Girls*—the show was about a month out from its second season premiere—was airing that random Saturday afternoon. It was hot and I was already lying down, so I just let it happen to me.

And I learned how wrong I'd been.

The show was fast and funny, sharp and emotional. Set in the cartoonishly small town of Stars Hollow, Connecticut, its centre was the mother-daughter duo Lorelai and Rory Gilmore (technically Rory's name is also Lorelai, in the tradition of men naming their sons after themselves—it's a key facet of the show's feminism, which is wildly variant). In the pilot we learn that the very smart Rory has just been accepted into a fancy private school that Lorelai cannot afford, forcing her to return to the family home she fled when she became pregnant at sixteen. Her parents, Emily and Richard, make her an offer: they'll pay for Rory's school, but the girls have to come to dinner at their house every Friday night. Lorelai, who wants her daughter to achieve her lifelong dream of a Harvard education, begrudgingly—like the most grudge that has ever be'd—accepts. And across the course of the show it uncorks their family issues, historical trauma, and new crises.

So, this show called *Gilmore Girls* was actually about three generations of the same family of women. Sure, there were Rory's idiot boyfriends (I am always and forever on Team Choose Yourself), and Lorelai's will they/won't they relationship with local restaurateur Luke, and the girls' respective careers, but it was about these three women. Their complicated, intense, dramatic, ever-changing relationships with each other. Outside of soap operas, I had never seen anything like it on television.

Gilmore Girls was created by Amy Sherman-Palladino, who cut her teeth as a writer on *Roseanne* at twenty-four years old. It was in that writers' room where she learned the mantra that has guided her television career: "Make the big small, and the small big." In other words, it's people, not plot.

She has made two more series—there was also a brief and woefully misguided traditional three-camera sitcom starring Parker Posey and Lauren Ambrose, *The Return of Jezebel James*, which didn't even air all its filmed episodes—in the *Gilmore* framework. There is *The Marvelous Mrs. Maisel*, about a New York woman in the 1950s who becomes an unlikely stand-up comedian, currently streaming; and a single season of *Bunheads*, about a woman who ends up running a dance school in a small, Stars Hollow–esque town, from 2012.

We meet all of Sherman-Palladino's heroes at a crossroads: Lorelai Gilmore has given her daughter a good life on her own terms, but now those terms aren't good enough for the next stage. *Bunheads*'s Michelle Simms is a fading and frustrated Vegas dancer who, through an unlikely series of events (a quickie marriage to a guy who immediately dies), ends up with an entire property in California and a chance to change her life's path, but she must forsake her dreams. (Dreams, their longtime existence and imminent extinguishing, figure prominently in A.S.P. 's worlds.) And Miriam "Midge" Maisel is a typical affluent '50s housewife—a great selection of hats, a nanny for her children, no job, and a husband who leaves her for his secretary. Her decision to pursue stand-up comedy is not just in defiance of her own family's social status, but of the times themselves.

These women are all stand-ins for their creator, who is a small, dark-haired hat aficionado, former dancer, and daughter of Catskills comedians. They're brunette, thin, and warm, in the form of: Lauren Graham, who bumped around sitcoms in the '90s before landing Lorelai; Broadway triple threat Sutton Foster as Michelle; and frequent dramatic series guest Rachel Brosnahan, who is naturally blond but dyed brown for Maisel. They're fast-talking dames of the *His Girl Friday* variety, with decades-spanning pop-culture references, great taste in music, and many opinions on food. They're bad at relationships because they can't just turn around and pick the guy (it's always a guy) who's been waiting patiently. They all have mommy issues—as daughters, and as mothers themselves, sometimes de facto in either case, but just as important.

Gilmore Girls was a success, as WB dramas in the 2000s go—it ran for seven seasons and had a devoted audience. A new, much bigger audience discovered it in 2015 when the series was picked up by Netflix. *Maisel*, which has streamed for four seasons on Amazon Prime, is high-rated and has won both Emmy and Golden Globe Awards, things that eluded the just-as-good *Gilmore Girls. Bunheads* was, confoundingly, a flop. Sutton Foster is a national treasure! It had Emily Gilmore (Kelly Bishop, as a lady named Fanny) in it too! Fuck the *Gilmore* reboot (wholly terrible, I will not mention it again), give us more *Bunheads*!

There are glaring flaws in Sherman-Palladino's world, too: Her heroes are often profoundly awful to those around them, quipping loudly through speeches, conversations, and movies. Even though there are some clearly queer-coded characters— Taylor and Michel on *Gilmore*, Susie on *Maisel*, maybe Sasha on *Bunheads*—no one is ever gay. (Rory and her frenemy, Paris, have a Spring Break kiss that's so chaste and uncomfortable it would make any performative girl-girl nightclub makeout you've ever seen look like an episode of *The L Word* by comparison.) Her towns are largely white—*Bunheads*'s detractors decried the lack of Black ballet dancers; without the singer Shy Baldwin, *Maisel*'s New York would look like *Gilmore*'s Connecticut.

She loves short, rat-faced, irredeemable men and insists on building stories around them, like *Gilmore*'s Jess (a pseudo-punk loser with commitment issues) and Midge Maisel's ex-husband, Joel (way too confident for someone that unfunny). Even though her shows are deeply emotional, Sherman-Palladino is unromantic to the point of coldness—see Luke telling Lorelai "I'm in. I am all in" instead of "I love you." Amateur theatre productions portray winter more authentically than either of her shows set on the east coast.

There are not one but two teen marriages on *Gilmore*, and when Rory's TEENAGE BFF, Lane, gets pregnant on her WEDDING NIGHT—she declares she'll never have sex again, and this is before she knows about the twins—not once does abortion come up, even though it would have been Rory's first thought, plus Lane's entire character is based on deviating from her strict Seventh-day Adventist upbringing.

She's also prone to a tasteless, pointless fat joke, as is her husband, Daniel Palladino, a longtime *Family Guy* writer—which means exactly what you think it does. (If there's an especially caustic, off-putting, deeply mean episode of an A.S.P. joint, I guarantee Daniel wrote it.)

Even with all this, and the fact that she often comes off like a real dick in interviews, I love Amy. Other than *Thelma & Louise*, no piece of cultural product has had as much effect on me as an artist as *Gilmore Girls*. The standard scriptwriting rule is one page equals one minute of film, which would make a network hour (with commercials) forty-five minutes, and pages, long. Sherman-Palladino's Gilmore scripts were usually eighty pages. The production hired a dialect coach for Alexis Bledel, who played Rory in her first-ever acting job at sixteen, so she could handle the pace of the dialogue. Some thought Amy was Aaron Sorkin writing under a pseudonym—ah yes, Sorkin, that famously nuanced depictor of the feminist perspective, who had one of the two girl characters in *The Social Network* set a garbage can on fire in a fit of hysteria—because surely a woman couldn't be this smart, this savvy, this dexterous a television writer.

In 2006, The WB tried to renegotiate the Palladinos' deal and failed, so the duo walked for the seventh and final season. But not before sabotaging the show with a secret tween daughter for Luke and shoving Lorelai into a doomed relationship with her shitty ex, Christopher. Rather than go quietly and respectfully as the network likely wanted, Amy instead blew up her own spot at the expense of people she'd worked with for six years.

I hated what it did to the show creatively—though it is one of the few series to ever have a finale that works—but I love that she did it. That attitude and that move are probably why she bonked around for the next ten years failing—sometimes deservedly, as with *Jezebel James*; sometimes unfairly, as with *Bunheads*—until *Maisel*'s success. (It is notable that even though she walked out on the *Gilmore* team, many of those writers, directors, and actors followed A.S.P. to subsequent projects.)

I also love that though Sherman-Palladino women are always effervescent and witty and astute, they're also and often very unlikeable. (Flawed is the word we use for this, usually.) They talk too much, listen too little, actively choose the wrong things often just to piss someone off, and come from immense privilege they rarely recognize. When Rory, who has stopped speaking to Lorelai for some ridiculous reason, marches into her grandparents' house to "make a deal," she is literally just asking them to pay for her Ivy League college tuition, which she knows they will do, because they have just paid for four years of her private high school education. But since she asked and not her mom, to her it's some huge symbol of independence and adulthood. It's actually, to anyone in the 99 percent, outlandish and ridiculous. Fuck you, Rory! (See? Unlikeable!)

When I began writing little one-act plays and eventually full-length screenplays, I took Amy's big/small credo with me, as well as her propensity for long, chatty scenes. In Stars Hollow there were often long, single-shot walk-and-talks, and when I wrote certain scenes I envisioned them being filmed like those. Alas, we couldn't afford a dolly on *Compulsus*. Nonetheless, the film has three dialogue scenes that run between five and six minutes, and were also the pages I used to audition the leads (might as well paint a verbose picture). Once my editor said she'd tried to trim down one of them, but she couldn't find a place to cut, because the writing all connected. I just shrugged, and smugly.

I'm also a big believer in saying less, taking lines away; that silence in the hands of the right actor can say more than six pages ever could, and Amy believes that too, which is why her very well-written shows are also incredibly well-cast. For every quotable one-liner or dazzlingly cut back-and-forth there's a heartbreaking, dialogue-free reaction shot that conveys just as much, probably more.

In an overcrowded television landscape I gave up on years ago—there's too much content, too many streaming services—I love that a voice like Amy's still appears every year or two like a beacon of brash, brassy, ballsy feminism. Her worst episode is better than the average series' best, and she delights and irritates in equal measure a lot of the time, which means her shows may be frustrating but are never boring. Her viewpoint is specific, her voice is singular, and her shows are uniquely, thrillingly hers. Though the plots stay small, the set-pieces can be huge: see the weekly dance sequences in *Bunheads*, the numerous themed festivals in Stars Hollow, and—among musical numbers and stand-up acts in grand settings, including a USO show that takes place in an aircraft carrier—the synchronized swimming scene in *Maisel*, clearly the show she's had the biggest budget on.

In the striving to fill all these streaming hours, television has become largely rote and generic. Tap into a franchise here or a reboot there, perhaps the year's prestige drama. Solemnly slog through it, tweet about it for a week, and move on like it never happened. Because of the sheer amount of Marvel and *Star Wars* content, all of those spinoff series have to fit within a grand master franchise plan, so they all look and sound the same. And television auteurs, who write every episode of a season, have always been men.

But Amy Sherman-Palladino, like Midge Maisel, is from another era. Her shows, to me at least, still feel special (especially since Amazon Prime lets her swear). And, curiously, she has no imitators. Is that the fault of a system that still doesn't really want to hand women the reins, especially if they're just gonna make shows about themselves? Is it because she's one of the last of the traditional network cohorts, who does things in a dying way? Or is it because no one would dare try?

ME ME ME
(MY MY MY)

THE GIRL BASSIST (MY FIRST BAND)

When I was in grade 6 my favourite show was *Jem*.

It was a cartoon about a woman named Jerrica who owned a record label and also ran a group home for girls (?) and *also* through some sort of synth magic led a double life as a pop star named Jem. She had stardom-infused earrings that were connected to a holographic computer named Synergy, and when she wanted to convert to Jem she would touch them and say "Showtime, Synergy!" and then there would be a musical number. A true genre-mashing feminist touchstone.

Jerrica also had a handsome boyfriend named Rio, and to this day I do not know if Rio knew she was also Jem, and neither does Google.

Jem's band was called The Holograms and they had punk rivals called The Misfits ("our songs are better")—there actually is a famous band called The Misfits, so this is weird—and they were always trying to undermine The Holograms. That was the most exciting part of the show to me—not the teen empowerment stuff, not the mystery of Jem's identity, not Rio or any other man—the two girl groups trying to best each other with totally banging singles. (I did not know at the time that it was a Hasbro-produced show created to sell dolls. Such is life.)

In grade 6 I was eleven, half-assedly playing the violin after ejecting myself out of piano lessons. But I couldn't *really* play anything, it's not like I was some sort of violin prodigy. I loved singing but it was not...encouraged. With all this and zero fashion sense, still—and because of Jem—I wanted to join a band.

In 2007, when I was twenty-eight, I did.

*

It borders on shocking to think of what a rage-filled, humourless harpy I am now, in my forties, and to consider that I didn't think I could be a band until a man gave me permission to.

I'd bought an acoustic guitar for myself on my eighteenth birthday in 1998, a beautiful Art & Lutherie from the Halifax Folklore Centre on Brunswick Street downtown. I knew a few chords and would occasionally attempt to learn songs—The Weakerthans's "Left and Leaving," some *Under Rug Swept*-era Alanis—but I didn't pursue music in any kind of way for another decade.

In the fall of 2007 I quit my full-time job at *The Coast* (the first time), because freelance was going well enough that it felt safe to. (Lurking recession: LOL!!!) One October afternoon of my free life, I needed batteries or something and went to The Source, a store I hate with my whole heart. (It goes: Long & McQuade, The Source, and Canadian Tire in descending order of worstness.) Terrible, condescending service. I've never seen a woman working at a Source.

But I was destined to bear it that day because it turned out there was a very shitty Ion electric guitar—a cheap Strat ripoff in sunburst, the most basic of guitar colours—as well as a tiny 15-watt amp and all the accessories, on sale for $30. THIRTY DOLLARS. It was the floor model of one of those all-in-one kits for parents to buy their kids, usually a couple hundred bucks, and here was me with no job wanting it instead.

The Source doink, sighing: "I'm gonna have to box this all up."

Me: "Well, let's do it."

He did, reluctantly, and I cabbed home, a luxury.

The guitar sucked—thin strings, bad action, tight-ass tuning pegs. But it was mine and I had something to plug it into. I was obsessed for a few weeks, then it fell away as the old-ass floor-model display strings snapped one by one. I didn't know how to change strings! Or write songs. And I had no one to play with.

Early the following year my friend Matt, who I'd met when I edited him at *The Coast* and of whom I was a longtime fan, asked me if I'd like to play bass in his band.

Me: Sure, but you know I don't...play the bass, right?

Matt: That's exactly what I want.

*

Here's what no one tells you about being in a band, especially at the beginning: It's fucking *expensive*.

You need your instrument (guitar, for our purposes. People tend not to take up the drums for the hell of it). You need an amplifier. Both of those things can be very cheap or wildly expensive and other musicians are very snobby about it. Then you need a tuning pedal ($100), and effects pedals ($50–$400, times however many you want to have), a pedalboard to arrange them all on for easy carry/accessibility ($50+), daisy chains to link your pedals' power together ($20-ish, these are always problematic), a power cord for the pedalboard (the common one is a 1 SPOT, they start at $30), tweener cords between each pedal ($20 for a handful), patch cords (two minimum, $20–$50 each), a capo ($30+), strings ($8), and picks ($1 each).

Just to play ONE fucking electric guitar.

Then there is the economics of being in a band. For the one I joined in 2008, Bloodsport, there was a monthly rehearsal-space fee, then we made a record (studio time, post-production time, vinyl printing), and then we toured (gas, hotels), and we made T-shirts and buttons to sell. We got a couple grants, and usually the money we made playing shows was enough to cover the rest of it—none of us were taking a salary, as it were—but upfront costs were out-of-pocket.

Everything I know about being in a band I learned in Bloodsport. I loved it. But it was *expensive*, and I was *unemployed*. And you can probably guess this already, but let me confirm that driving from Halifax to Fredericton immediately after everyone gets off work to play for forty minutes at 12:30 a.m. to make $60 to split among four people is not math that works in anyone's favour.

*

The bass unlocked some music theory in me I hadn't considered since I'd jammed on the violin all those years ago. It was melodic, but it was also rhythmic—it bridged the gap between guitars and the drums. (This is common knowledge, but it wasn't to me.)

Weirdly, those four strings made me understand the mechanics of music in a way I never had before, very likely not because no one had attempted to teach me but because I simply hadn't been paying attention.

So I started writing songs. On the *bass*. A single note at a time. Which is very ironic if you consider my predilection toward guitar solos now (zero). The downstroke post-rock of Bloodsport meant I was already playing the bass like a rock guitar—strums not patterns—and the songs I was struggling to construct fit into this style well.

It's a particular thing, to be a girl bassist in a band. Think D'arcy Wretzky then Melissa Auf der Maur in The Smashing Pumpkins, or Kims Deal (Pixies) and Gordon (Sonic Youth). You stand out. You add diversity, even when you're straight and white, like those women are. (I was white and closeted, so same.) People booking festivals are like "cool, there's a lady bassist" and think it counts as diversity even though every bandleader is a straight white man (women and non-binary people FRONTING the band counts the most, don't be obtuse).

Most sound technicians are men and they came up in a scene that is not kind to not-men—it's called the music industry—and they usually think you're a real band guy's girlfriend, or if not that, during sound check they ask your bandmate what you'd like in the monitor, or they ask where your bandmate is when they've got your band's cut of the money at the end of the night. (That's what you get for being the lady bass player and not the frontperson. Frontman.)

I don't even think it's active misogyny, just run-of-the-mill garbage that's so ingrained they don't even notice they're doing it. If it's not a sound guy, it's a member of the touring or opening band saying shit out of the side of their mouth about your gear or fiddling with your pedals on your behalf after you've strummed one (1) chord. You also didn't ask to use their guitar or amp, which is better than yours of course so here take it, even though it weighs fifteen pounds and they don't know your band's music and have not heard you play or sing a word. You certainly didn't ask your own guitarist to get into some weird dick-swinging fight about the amp the other guitarist brought, then take twenty minutes out of the night to go get his, which (again) is better, says him. (No one ever asks you your opinion, which is obviously stupider than every man's in the building, even the bartender's, so why would it matter.)

I was the girl bassist in a band for three years and I loved it but part of me also hated it. I had enough self-esteem issues, I didn't need to add "dismissed/ignored cause men don't want to bang me" to the list. If there had been a way to walk in, play the show, and walk out, I would have done it. But so much of being in a band, other than the cost, is the lugging of the shit and the waiting around. You're just amongst these awkward antisocial dudes, some of whom know each other and stick together, and some who see each other as competition and create weird pseudo-rivalries. They are often *quite* unwashed (and they will have a girlfriend and I won't!). It's stale and unpleasant.

I took the songs I'd been writing and started my own project. I sang on only one song in Bloodsport—not because anybody had stopped me, it just didn't occur to me to express that I wanted to—but I had my own feelings to voice. It was much gentler, and in standard tuning.

My good friend Danny, in a band for years, had recently started to do his own thing too. He had a solo show at the local folk club and he kindly asked me to open it. (I still needed a man's permission to do my shit. For the record I do not blame the men for this; without Matt and Danny I wouldn't even play music.)

I asked my friend Kinley to play violin on the five songs I'd written, plus a cover of Death Cab For Cutie's "Marching Bands of Manhattan" to get to a full half-hour set. We were both so nervous for the first practice that we sat back to back on a small couch in her kitchen, not even able to look at one another. I'd never been so artistically vulnerable with another human being before. I called us Dance Movie, after my favourite film genre.

The show went...well? I'd gotten over the bulk of my stage fright thanks to Bloodsport, but this was different—me in the front, two of us instead of four. Fewer things to look at. The room was packed. I had a sweet borrowed guitar from my friend Jenn. I'd been covering musicians, kindly and with enthusiasm, for a decade as a journalist, and they gave it right back to me. I'll never forget looking to the bar and seeing a line of the day's most prominent artists staring back at me, engaged and smiling. Even if it was all for show (it wasn't), it felt amazing and inspiring.

The band evolved from that night. Kinley and I did a few shows together, then we added the first of many Dance Movie drummers, Craig. (Shoutout Tynan, Denise, Rebecca, Pinky, Glen, and Sean!) Kinley ultimately bowed out to be in a little outfit called Hey Rosetta! permanently, and the lineup shifted around me until it settled on Pinky (Josh) and Trevor, drums and bass respectively.

We knew each other from the internet and around Halifax, but they were from Yarmouth, a tiny town at the most southwestern point of Nova Scotia. They'd been playing music together their whole lives, which is what you want in a drummer and a bassist—they need to be in sync, simpatico. Their roots were in dank post-rock, dramatic instrumental outfits like Sigur Rós and Explosions in the Sky, and the oddly delicate songwriting of their hometown heroes Brian Borcherdt and Paul Murphy of Wintersleep, who happened to be two of my songwriting inspirations.

Against some odds, the three of us got on like a house on fire. Our practices and shows were dynamic and thrilling. Other musicians had made the first Dance Movie record, *Interlopers*, with me, but Trevor and Josh played the release show in 2012. (So did Rebecca, who's been in and out over the years, and as of this writing is in. She had taken over Kinley's violin parts but soon ditched those strings for lead guitar, and we're grungier for it.) We travelled to North by Northeast in Toronto together and kicked ass at two shows that got us written up as a top 10 new act in *Now* at the end of the festival.

It always takes me a long time but I started writing new songs—every song is a miracle, not of artistry but of existence—and eventually I had enough to make another record. At that time I was in my early thirties, invigorated by my band, and still had hope for my musical future. I'd seen bands make records with semi-famous Canadian musicians producing—Hawksley Workman was a big one at the time—and I thought, boring. We can do something different.

John Goodmanson had made the best Sleater-Kinney record, *Dig Me Out*, and as it turned out, their secret comeback record, *No Cities to Love*, which he finished before he came to Nova Scotia from his home in Seattle. I footed much of the five-figure bill by working a tonne that year and quitting doing anything fun at all (no drinks for six months). Somehow, I pulled it all together, flew John in, and we made *Pierce* in five days on the south shore.

It took three more years to put it out—I got very, very sad and it paralyzed me, I couldn't do anything—but that release show in 2017 and the record itself are two of my top artistic achievements. Most of the vinyl is still in my closet and we never toured it or got a review in a high-profile publication, but it's the best thing I've ever made, and it's the best experience I've had making something.

All this happened because I'd quit my job ten years earlier.

I'm not a positive person and I don't have much faith in the world, but there has been no time I've taken a risk that hasn't paid off. If not literally—never literally!—at least artistically, or emotionally. I wish I could remember this on my lowest days, my go-nowhere days, those stagnant days that are grey and familiar and it seems like nothing will ever change. It can if you want it.

And I'm here to tell you *not* to follow my path: Do not wait for anyone to give you permission. Don't waste years wondering. Throw this book into the fucking sea and go do it.

THE MAN-HATING DYKE
(MY VIGILANTE MOVIE)

The path to getting *Compulsus* made begins with a cliché.

In 2019, I turned forty. Two months previous I'd left the company I'd been with for my whole adult life, and it ended badly. The morning of my birthday I was on an interminable call with Employment Insurance for the first time ever, having already messed it up but not having any idea how. At my party that night a married person drunkenly pitched me, relentlessly and without a single reasonable argument or support materials, that we become girlfriends as if it were a flawless, air-tight idea.

What was this life? I didn't like it.

I'd had a short film idea bonking around for years—a battered woman shows up at another woman's house, and that woman immediately leaves and does something very violent to the man who perpetrated it. A single tracking shot, no dialogue.

I'd parked it, as I often did. But I had lots of free time on the horizon. And a few significant things had happened:

1: Seth MacFarlane hosted the Academy Awards

Billionaire idiot Seth MacFarlane, creator of the frat-boy *The Simpsons* rip-off *Family Guy* and other even worse *Family Guy* rip-offs, hosted the Oscars in 2013.

He opened with a song called "We Saw Your Boobs," high-lighting a bunch of women—including actual Oscar winners Kate Winslet, Meryl Streep, and Penélope Cruz—who'd done nudity on film. The camera cut to each actor as he sang about them. They all reacted gamely, because these were the dying days of women being "good sports" who could "take a joke." Some even pre-recorded their reactions, which is sadder/more infuriating.

The spark of my feminist vengeance was lit with this ludi-crous fucking song.

2: Jian Ghomeshi's trial

I knew Jian professionally—in 2005 I'd been a guest on a CBC Radio show of his, *The National Playlist*, and afterwards he'd written me a beautiful email with a top 10 of his favourite things and I was on the list. (This would become notable later.) I was one of only three repeat guests in the show's final weeks the fol-lowing year.

He came to Halifax for some reason and we went to dinner—not a date, he was sure to tell me once he saw me in person for the first time—and a Matt Mays show. He told me about how he'd been planning to move to New York when *Playlist* ended—"I had an apartment on hold and everything"—but CBC had just given him his own show, and I'd be on it.

He kept his word, and I got a couple years of freelance out of *Q*. Then the recession happened, things got very bad for me, and by 2009 *Q* had stopped using me. (Freelance budgets are always the first thing to go.) Jian's star continued to rise. He wrote a book. He would do things like go to the UK to see David Bowie and sell stories to the *Globe and Mail* about it. Sometimes I would see him at CBC HQ in Toronto when I would record my Halifax and New Brunswick radio hits from TIFF, but we didn't have any kind of relationship.

I was in a movie theatre one Sunday afternoon in late October 2014, down in the basement of Halifax's Park Lane Mall. My phone didn't work in the building at all. It was dark as I slowed on the corner of South Park Street, and my pocket started buzzing repeatedly as my service returned. Knowing what was going to happen on Monday, Jian had made a pre-emptive Facebook post about how he liked rough sex and the prudes at CBC were upset at him for it.

The rest of the story is available elsewhere, but if you're reading this book you probably already know it. It turned out I knew two of his three accusers, though not well, and one was a sharp and funny firecracker I'd worked with directly that first year at *Q*, the same year during which Jian had told her, in the office, he wanted to hate-fuck her over a desk.

It's hard to explain how that story galvanized a certain strain of Canadian women, and I don't think this is me being self-involved for once. When that trial was going on, when CBC produced a wan *Fifth Estate* episode in late March 2016—how could the network that created this environment possibly produce an unbiased program about it, also: *what the fuck*?!—everyone I knew was obsessed with it. Lucy DeCoutere, one of his accusers, was a local actor and she was being eviscerated on the stand. We felt personally connected to this major national story in a way we usually weren't, and it dredged up a lot of shit for a lot of people. That's what happens when you pick a scab.

The hardest part for me was learning how many of my friends were sexual assault survivors, as some of them dealt with that trauma for the first time in years, if ever. (And oddly I felt guilty for cruising through life mostly unscathed.) I have a distinct memory, after multiple brutal days of Lucy's testimony, of returning home from my weekly CBC hit at 9:00 A.M. and climbing back into bed fully clothed, unable to bear any of it anymore.

3: Me Too

Tarana Burke founded the Me Too movement in 2006, but I didn't see it until a random day in 2017, when people started posting #MeToo on Facebook, which had been ported over from Twitter during Harvey Weinstein's rape trial. That hashtag meant the person posting had been sexually assaulted in some way.

I think men were confused and thought every hashtag meant "raped," not realizing that basically every woman they knew had been harassed or hurt in some way. It's a staggering statistic to be faced with when it doesn't happen to you (or when you are the perpetrator of it); like so much patriarchal bullshit, they think that because it's happened to everyone it couldn't possibly have happened to anyone, as if we all just want to be hurt for the fucking sake of it.

Soon Weinstein fell. Then Bill Cosby, finally. Woody Allen, kind of. But they were not brought down by Facebook—the highest echelons of the press were needed to do it, *The New York Times* and *The Atlantic* and *New York Magazine* and *The New Yorker*. Which meant every week, it seemed, there was some deeply upsetting, meticulously reported, wholly awful piece to read written by top-notch reporters. With Cosby the survivors were regular people, with Weinstein they were a shocking number of celebrities.

No one was safe, and it took decades—until age and relevance came for these men, when it was safe for the rest of the sycophants to join the cause du jour—to bring them to any kind of justice.

4: Park jerk-off

After four movies and well over ten thousand steps midway through the Toronto International Film Festival in 2018, I took a shortcut through a sketchy park to my hotel. I was intercepted by a pantsless man, masturbating and aiming straight for me, a dead-eyed giant. I was unable to speak, but I stepped wide enough away from him that he changed direction and went off into the bushes.

The park was full and a lot of people saw, and nobody helped me. (Sincerely and forever, fuck you, Toronto.) I felt guilty that he had just gone and done it to someone else; I felt lucky that nothing like this had happened to me until right now, at thirty-eight; mostly I felt a radical, roiling rage. Later the skies opened in that sudden violent way they do in Ontario, and I thought, *GOOD. I hope you fucking get pneumonia and die.*

This was my *Falling Down* moment.

∗

So, as I was saying, I turned forty in 2019.

I was officially middle-aged and I had no job, no girlfriend, and half a life's worth of taking barely any chances. It was time to change at least one, ideally all, of those things.

The week I turned forty, the Atlantic Filmmakers' Co-operative (AFCOOP) in Halifax announced an inaugural workshop facilitated by Iain MacLeod called *writing small*: The goal was to help writers create scripts specifically with a micro-budget in mind for Telefilm's Talent to Watch program, which awarded up to twenty-five first-time Canadian feature film directors and producers $150,000 to make a movie. (It's $250,000 now.)

You could apply to AFCOOP's workshop with three ideas and I sent two—an adaptation of a largely plotless short story by a much better writer than me, and one about a lady vigilante who beats up men at night. If I recall correctly the jury did not recommend the latter, but Iain wanted me to do it, and I wanted to do it, so that's what we developed in the workshop.

At first it was called *Misandrist*, which I thought was funny, like "Jessica Chastain is *Miss Andrist*, the ginger suffragette history never dared tell you about!" It became *Compulsus* in the first draft stage through a boring Google rabbit hole. "Compulsus" means "striking together; hostile." It's also a love story.

In my two decades as a journalist I have never written an outline. Same goes for the three features I'd written previously—

I'm psychotically chronological; I need to start at the start and end at the end. I can move things around later, but the writing is all linear. Iain and the workshop showed me what a wasteful process that can be—by the time I was ready to write a draft in December of 2019 I had it all in order, which is the point. I was free to hop around and write the parts I did know, even if I didn't know the part that came before them yet. This is common knowledge, but here I was learning it now.

I kept saying, very pretentiously, "This movie seems to want to be written at night." So I wrote it in the light of the Christmas tree, listening to Lana Del Rey, drinking Tannen Bomb beer from Hell Bay in Shelburne, which is a co-production with the Christmas Tree Council of Nova Scotia that really tastes like pine needles, even though I think it's made with fir boughs. (There is not an ounce of the holidays in *Compulsus*.) The story is very simple, easily outline-able in fact: Wally, a poet and freelance writer fed up with hearing tales of hipster male abuse from people she cares about, takes it upon herself to start taking out the bad men. The first one's an accident, the rest are not. She's also starting a new relationship with a woman named Lou and trying to keep her new hobby a secret. But guess what, she can't!

In February 2020 Nicole Steeves came on as the producer—people are surprised to learn now that we didn't know each other then, but we didn't. She'd been part of a film festival Q&A I once conducted; I have no memory of speaking to her otherwise. I knew she was sharp and funny. She was stuck in a bizarre funding purgatory so to produce a Talent to Watch would be to advance her own career as a writer-director. Worked for me! We forged an awkward alliance. (Now we are close.)

In March, Women in Film and Television–Atlantic nominated the project to Telefilm (the Talent to Watch process is long and convoluted), one week before that other thing happened in March.

Telefilm's timelines were knocked off by the Covid-19 pandemic but in the end, we got it—we found out in July 2020 and we went to camera March 18, 2021, almost exactly one year later. Now I had a team of twenty—mostly women, by the way, and they were not hard to find, *by the way*—carrying out my revenge fantasies. There were but two men on set (Nicole would not let me call them Boy 1 and Boy 2).

The idea had changed over time: the target wasn't some random jerk-off in a park (though we did encounter one during our shoot, more in a minute), it was the men in my artistic community who led double lives as public feminist allies and private abusers of feminists. "S-o-f-t-b-o-i-s," as I spelled it for a nervous dude walking by one of our night shoots, probably regretting asking after the plot.

Because we had multiple stunts where one person was assaulting another on a city street, often with a weapon, on those nights we had to hire police officers. They shut down the street and everything, parking their cruiser across the end. It felt major—and, I will add, other than a group of drunk buffoons walking by and yelling, "They're shootin' a movieeeeeee," we had no trouble when the police were with us.

We also had plenty of night shoots that didn't have stunts, and those nights were considerably more difficult. A film crew, even a small one like ours, is both very obvious and not very mobile. If you're filming somewhere, you're clearly *there*. There's gear and sandbags and people and a snack area. And if you're on the street and don't have the police around, no one has to listen to you. If they're in your shot, you have no authority to move them. They do not care about your street permit, which only permits you to shoot on the street, not control it.

It was not lost on me then nor is it now that every disruption we had came from a man on the street. Here are my top three, in order of annoying to horrible:

1 We had the street fully, properly, officially shut down in a residential neighbourhood, with a line of five women stretched across it, chanting. Yet a man still drove through the line—again, IN THE MIDDLE OF THE STREET—on his bicycle, while one of the city guys chased him, yelling. Reader, we did not get the shot.

2 Wally and Lou have their first kiss outside a restaurant, after a date. I'd picked the location, the corner of Portland Place and Gottingen Street, but reconsidered a couple weeks out because there's a Salvation Army across the street. I wasn't worried about the men who lived there causing trouble on the set, but I was worried about them gawking at two women making out, repeatedly.

We shot it there anyway—it backed onto the next location, and so often with filmmaking you're just trying to make things as simple as you can—and my instinct, to no one's surprise, turned out to be right. (For extra fun, two men decided to do some boxing training while we were shooting, literally punching a practice bag with actual boxing gloves. We left the background sound of the street cacophony in the scene, since it really underscored the movie's entire point.)

3 Wally's apartment location was on the corner of this sweet alcove of Halifax's north end that had a handful of tiny streets with very little traffic. In the film's climax—no spoilers—Wally has to run across town in the middle of the night. We decided to shoot her running on each of the streets surrounding us; there were enough to make it look as long as the journey needed to be. (Movies are nothing but lies.)

We shot the first segment no problem and were setting up the second in what amounted to an alley behind Wally's apartment. I could hear tinny music coming from somewhere—I scanned the area and dread crept over me when I realized someone was staring back at me from the shadows at the end of a driveway.

We all realized at the same time that there was a new presence on set. A large, silent man ambled into the middle of our group. He had face tattoos, some bags hanging off his shoulders, a weird doll strapped across himself, a tiny radio blasting the music—I don't remember what it was—and an incredibly volatile energy. It's one of those things that's hard to relay when you're telling the story later, the way he stared and how it felt like he could explode at any moment.

Our wonderful assistant director, Melani, said, kindly but with a tough note in her voice, "We're making a movie, if you wouldn't mind moving along?" He silently raised a peace sign at her, at all of us. She tried again to get him to move along. He wouldn't look her in the face or say anything. Some people remember him grunting, but I must have blocked it out.

Then he started touching himself outside his pants. People started to scatter.

I looked around, starting to freak out, thinking, "Ok, who's going to take care of this?" And then it dawned on me: *No one.* There were two very young men on set, and that was it. It's one of the few times in my life I wanted an ass-kicker dude to deploy within arm's reach. There were nearly two dozen of us, and en masse we ran into the apartment's backyard and locked the gate, to escape this single idiot.

Nicole herded us all into the house and called the police. They came quickly but immediately dismissed our fears: "Oh yeah, we know that guy. He's harmless." (Cool story! They were not the ones who'd been on set with us.)

The cruiser lights had sent him scurrying so we went back to the alley. We shot one take, then he came ambling back. At that point it was 10:00 P.M., we only had an hour left on the clock and it was clear it was going to be more stressful than productive. Melani smartly and swiftly shut us down for the night.

This kind of shit is part of what enraged me enough to write the movie in the first place, so I guess it was at least a sign we were on the right track. (I will never shoot on a Halifax street again.)

*

As I'm writing this, *Compulsus* is on the film festival circuit. We've got plans and dreams of varying degrees, but who knows where we'll end up. By the time this book is in your hands it'll be available to the public in some capacity. There will have been some reaction to it by now, though I can't predict what size or scope.

But I do know this is the first time—possibly this book is the second—I have taken the cumulative microaggressions I've weathered, alongside the greater crimes endured by survivors all around me, and turned them into art (with a $200,000 budget!). I'm knocking on my mid-forties now, and I'm in one of the best career cycles of my life, so it's also the first time living a cliché has worked in my favour.

For clichés are rooted in truth. And the truth will set you down a vengeful path to feminist righteousness. Eventually.

INDEPENDENT CHRISTMAS
(MY FIRST HOLIDAY AWAY FROM HOME)

I n September of 2014, I entered some search terms into an app called Skyscanner.

Travelling from: Halifax
Travelling to: New York
Departure date: December 23, 2014
Return date: December 30, 2014

The price it spat back at me: $332.96

For years, I'd been working up the courage to leave at Christmas. My parents split up in January of 1998; that holiday season was horrible and poisoned me for the rest of my life (I turned thirty-six in 2014, so fully half of it by that point).

The shape of my family changed dramatically in those years, as families do. My sisters partnered up, moved and, as normal and regular contributors to society, got free passes not to come home.

But I—forever the single one, who had no in-laws or children—travelled back annually, faithfully, as expected. I did the dinners, the Christmas-light drives, the terrible television marathons. (I loathe you with all the rage of a pre-ghost Ebenezer Scrooge, *Big Bang Theory*.) Sometimes one of my sisters would be there, sometimes both, but a lot of it I did by myself.

The older I got the shorter I made my time at home, not because it was particularly terrible but because it was an obligation, which I resented. I also grew to resent the idea that my aloneness was seen as loneliness by others. "I just don't want you sitting by yourself in that apartment," my father would say. But I wanted to be there in my empty house: with my cats, full control of the television, trips to the liquor store whenever I wanted, access to good coffee, and all the time in the world.

No one ever asked me what I wanted. Nor did they relay exactly what my presence meant to them in the first place—we would usually run out of things to talk about on the drive from Halifax to my dad's place. It's not like there was a years-long stream of intellectual discourse we needed to dip back into. We tried to understand each other, got as far as we could, and gave up.

When that plane ticket appeared, cheap and on a pay week, I knew it was time. My father was upset, to say the least. I bore it and packed. It took me ten hours to get to New York—you want a deal? There are conditions—but at least I had comfort waiting.

I'd met Allison in the Halifax airport back in 2011, when she came to speak at Strategic Partners, an industry conference held as part of the Atlantic International Film Festival. I was mooching a ride on my way home from TIFF, and she was an official delegate. We ended up in the same shuttle and talked the whole way into the city. She works in film, has hair like Tami

Taylor and an apartment on the first Brooklyn stop of the 2/3 line. Clark Street is the tiniest piece-of-shit subway station you ever did see—no stairs, just a freight elevator—but it was one block from her place, which was two blocks from a whole bunch of stuff. "Lena Dunham lives in the neighbourhood," she noted. This year, she would be in her hometown in Rhode Island for the holidays, so her place was empty for the week.

On Christmas Eve I went to the movies. I kept asking store clerks how late they were open and they invariably said "twenty-four hours" because New York is not a small Canadian town run by uptight old white Christians. I told servers and workers about how the penny had been eliminated in my country, that all the American ones were weighing my wallet down, and literally no one gave a shit.

My wish to be by myself was coming true, and I floated around as the whims of the day allowed, though home tugged at me—that night I had an awkward phone call with my father, who was understandably hurt. "Please don't take it personally," I said, knowing full well there was no other way to take it. "I have no idea where you are or who you're with," he replied, as if that was something he ever knew when I was in Halifax.

On Christmas morning, I got more texts than I've ever gotten at the holidays. It was like people were making an extra effort because they thought I was going through something, even though to me it had been so long coming.

I felt very far from my own life. But wasn't that the point?

I built a goal into each day. I walked across the Brooklyn Bridge. I saw two Broadway shows and one had Michael Cera and I didn't even hate it. I went to four movies, including a

35mm version of *Inherent Vice* (ugh) at the Angelika and a screening of *Selma* at the Brooklyn Academy of Music, mere weeks after a round of anti-police protests had died down. In that predominantly Black neighbourhood, on Christmas Day, the audience wept and applauded individual screen credits. I visited The Strand. I went to the Brooklyn Flea. I hung out in a coffee shop called Sit & Wonder. I went to a rock show at Saint Vitus, where I connected with two friends also visiting from Nova Scotia, a great relief and a break from myself. We FaceTimed my sister from the back of a cab, then one of them took us to the bar of the bartender she'd picked up a few days earlier and we got cheap drinks.

By the time I was sitting on the floor of The Knitting Factory waiting for Hannibal Buress to come on stage, the weight of my aloneness was palpable. No matter how many things I did, I did them by myself. "Hey you, it's me, You! Still!" Hannibal brought out Chance the Rapper as a surprise and I was too tired to stay. A girl who'd been by herself near me at the bar was on the same subway platform as me and I considered saying something, desperate to make a connection, but I didn't.

It was trial by candlelight, that trip: I overestimated my need for solitude, but not its purpose. I posted a photo album, the easiest way to make it appear as if everything is great, and watched the Likes climb and the supportive messages pop up. I didn't crave outside validation, but it helped.

The problem was the trip was too damn long!

The next year I chose Chicago—ultimately I wanted to go to Berlin, but I don't live a life that can afford holiday vacations overseas, at least not up to this point—and I made it six days. This one, though shorter, was less successful.

I'd had a big personal blowout a few days before leaving, and I was a fucking mess. Sometimes I wonder whether I would have changed everything in the course of that relationship if I'd just stayed home, but deep down I know it wouldn't have mattered. At the time, though, it was fraught and awful. The stress of it meant I was perpetually on my period at day-two strength—two weeks total, cool cool—and unable to talk to her very much because the apartment I was staying in didn't have Wi-Fi and in those days my data was limited. It was a real "wherever you go, there you are" cock-up.

The weather was awful for my whole time there, rainy and/ or cold, to the point where it stranded me in the city for an extra day after shutting down the entirety of the O'Hare airport, and *then* I got stranded at my connection point in Toronto the next day—after taking a 7:00 A.M. flight with a two-hour security line—and had to eat shit and ask my dad to get me a hotel room because I was out of money because the trip was two days longer than planned. (To his great credit, he was not a dick about it.)

Everything about Christmas in Chicago felt like punishment—for being ungrateful, or for daring to be happy against all logic and reason for one fucking night before I'd gone down there. There were times when life got in the way and you had to not take the trip, and this was one of them, so I was getting mine for doing it anyway. (The truth is the weather is bad in the middle of North America in December. The rest of it is not some grand penance. Shit happens.)

I took the following year off because Trump got elected, and went back to New York from Boxing Day to New Year's Eve the year after that because I needed to leave town. I did

Christmas Day then my dad drove me to the airport. It was a solid -20 degrees for the whole trip, but I finally hit the sweet spot of Independent Christmas: Not too long, no personal strife, reasonable expectations, from both my family *and* me.

The years have been complicated following that third year in New York—there has been illness and loss and now a pandemic. Regardless, I no longer feel the need to flee the country, nor do I feel like I have to park myself in East Hants out of some old obligation. I stay in the city, go to the movies, visit friends for dinner, call my dad, and it's all fine. I don't owe anybody anything. I never did.

THERE'S NOTHING LIKE A MAD WOMAN (MY VIRAL TWEET)

The older I become, and the more I understand what men are about (see *Compulsus* essay), the angrier I get.

One old trope became very evident to me when I was around thirty-five, and my single male peers began doing the thing men in that cohort (and way above) do—date women in their early- to mid-twenties.

They would pursue, attain, and forge some sort of relationship with a woman a solid dozen years younger than them. And it would last a few months, sometimes a year or two, then it would implode. I would hear the same thing in the wake of all of those breakups, even from men I considered good, empathetic feminists:

"She was crazy."

The first or second or fifth time I heard it I thought, "Well, *obviously*. Here's this guy, my friend, thirty-seven years old, doing his best! And this hipster student, not even alive during the first season of *Friends*, this *bitch*, she caused *drama* all the time?! He was trapped by her wily ways! Thank god he got out!!!!"

We all know this is bullshit, yet we have to come to it in our own time, because the patriarchy has structured it as such. It has (men have) made MAN the default voice of reason, of intent, of worth, of belief. Woman? Better get a second opinion!

Why do you think, when they are sexually assaulted, women have to detail every touch, word, drink, item of clothing, location, and person they told immediately after to be believed (and still *aren't*), and men just have to say "I didn't do it"?

Anyway, as mentioned in a previous essay, I was radicalized by the Jian Ghomeshi trial and the Harvey Weinstein accusations and Bill Cosby and the Catholic Church and and and, this absolute avalanche of trauma being unleashed directly toward a largely unsuspecting world, myself included. It was then I learned how many of the people I cared about were survivors. As far as I'd known we'd all been lucky, but that was not true, and I was ashamed by a naivety I thought I'd left in the country. I became consumed by the thought of all the pain people were carrying with them in their day-to-day lives, because this awful behaviour was so commonplace, and if everyone allowed themselves to be broken by it the world would grind to a halt. It was too much to expect of the average person, and here they all were doing it.

It was then I got infected by—invigorated by?—a constant, roiling rage. It was then I decided to stop taking men at face value simply because men told me I should.

So that meant things like sexual assault, very obviously. It meant less important but loud, pervasive things like opinions about art.

It also meant this "crazy bitch" shit. I started putting together that it was the same type of guy saying it, and saying it in the same kind of *aw, shucks* way, as if they couldn't believe it, it just snuck up on them, how crazy this bitch got suddenly.

I was thinking about all of this one random Thursday, a day like any other roiling-rage day, and I posted a tweet:

If a man calls his ex some form of "crazy" I am
immediately on her side even if I've never met her

This was before I got fired (for tweeting, in case you hadn't heard), so my account was open, which meant I was free to be liked more than 25,000 times, which is what happened.

Some people get 400 likes and go "I don't have a SoundCloud, but"—which is the most ridiculous fucking thing, it's not even funny—and then drop a link to something no one will ever go to. It's super weird, in the first place, that people think someone would read the SECOND tweet of a stranger, even with threading. People are lazy morons and they do not care about you.

You know how I know? Because the stats of my viral tweet amounted to over 1 million impressions. You know how many new followers I got? THREE.

Anyway, it was a solid few days of feeling like Lena Dunham. Random women loved it. Random dudes were pissed. They rarely replied to me directly, which I appreciated, they were just fighting amongst their friends. Things like:

"What about when she is crazy, though?"

[some bullshit description of a physical altercation that never happened]

"Not all men!"

All the types.

My friend Jacob, a lovely bisexual male feminist, couldn't believe the legs the tweet had. "Someone famous must have retweeted it." They hadn't, the sentiment was just that commonplace. (The actor-turned-writer, and Twitter celebrity, Mara Wilson eventually did.)

The furor died down within a couple days of course but once every month or two for years, until I locked up, I would get a random like on the viral tweet. (Probably, let's face it, from someone searching "crazy bitch.") It taught me a lot about the internet's short-term memory, which is approximately half a day long. This tips into a more recent idea that every day Twitter has a villain, and you don't want to be that day's villain, and that very few people consider the source or the context in which they see the tweet. It's just a retweet with added commentary through one's own lens.

In short, it reinforced some things I was already aware of: That people don't read critically. That men of any age cannot ably, successfully, or convincingly defend their predilections for younger women. That even when you're calling out gaslighting, many men will use your statement to...do some more gaslighting, and without an ounce of self-awareness or self-reflection. And that many women—thousands, in fact—know exactly what I was talking about.

I NEVER WANTED CHILDREN
(MY TRUTH)

I call myself "a late bloomer." My friend, the poet Sue Goyette, once said, "Yeah, you're breaking the system" of timelines that are really just marketing, which is a nice way to put it.

I am resistant to change: I had one job for nineteen years and another for (a mostly overlapping) fifteen; I've been in my current apartment for nine years and the one before that for eight years; I came out when I was in my late twenties; and I've wanted to make music since I was twelve and movies since I was sixteen but didn't start until I was twenty-eight and forty, respectively. I'm scared of everything and slow to come around on any of it.

But I have never wanted kids.

Part of it comes from being gay and grappling with that for an extra-long time, and just not understanding how the family unit, how motherhood, could work outside of the "normal" way. I had enough to worry about just within myself, there was no room for extension.

It seems outlandish and overdramatic now, but I put off dealing with being gay as long as I could simply because I didn't want it to be true, and sometimes saying it out loud still feels like a lie, because I didn't admit it for so long. I basically forced myself into an asexual space as I attempted to hide—I did like a couple boys I half-heartedly tried to date, but they were never interested, wonder why—and I planned to live my life just never addressing it.

I didn't want to be different.

I got over that eventually, obviously—there's nothing more boring to me now than a straight person, sorry for your loss. I have three nephews between my two sisters, but only a handful of my close friends have children, and I've felt a sense of dread with each pregnancy announcement because it meant there would be less of them for me. (My youngest sister, mother of two, once chided me for being that selfish.)

Another part of it comes down to my life choices. I worked at the same alternative weekly newspaper for nineteen years, which means I've made garbage money for my entire adult life. CBC paid me as much for eight minutes on air as the paper did in a full eight-hour workday, so when I did both, I did well, but I was part-time at the paper for nine years after nearly two away. So, all told I've really only made a reasonable—calling it good is laughable—salary for about four of my twenty-three working years. At one point I was a three-year tax delinquent, and that came back to bite me in the ass.

Now I've pivoted to that real cash grab, *microbudget filmmaking*!

The point is: Life is hard for me in that way. I have barely made it through certain years. I've never had a serious relationship—anyone to support me, which I would rather die than accept anyway—so it's been all me, all the time. Due to being a town with lots of universities and the only city east of Montreal, Halifax has always been expensive to live in, way more than it has any right to be considering its remote location, dismal transit system, and lack of amenities. Home ownership is not an option for me. I had a roommate until I was forty. The cats eat before I do.

To be responsible for someone else in the midst of all this? Hell the fuck no. The baby would have been orphaned young when I died of a stress-induced heart attack. I literally can't imagine that life, the same way I can't imagine being rich or, I don't know, being a trucker.

But being a parent is not the same thing as being of a certain class or having a certain job. Somehow the biological imperative of reproduction has never been turned on in me. (Maybe it will be, considering my bloomerness, but the window is already nearly closed so it's going to be too late.) There are lots of reasons people don't have babies—they didn't find the right partner, they can't for health reasons, they want to but their partner doesn't.

And some people just don't fucking want to. Sometimes I'll see an old friend or past-life person at a wedding or funeral and they'll ask me if I have kids and my reaction every time is laughter. Not just because of how I feel about it, but seriously, do I emanate mommy vibes to you??

I haven't had a relationship with my mother since I was twenty-five, and it bothers people enough that they express their opinion on it in a way they wouldn't about my weight or my ill-advised freelance career. People have told me to my face, often in the wake of their own loss, that I'll regret it once she's gone. After my best friend had her first child, she really started hammering me about it—"Are you ever going to talk to your mom?"—and I would shrug and she would talk about how devastated she would be if her son didn't speak to her.

Deadbeat dads are such an entrenched societal norm that if you swapped out the parent in my case, no one would even bat an eye—people expect dads to be shitty and subsequently cut out of lives. But mothers run deeper, even though many of the grown-ass women I know and love have endlessly fraught, awful relationships with theirs. It's nobody's business, just shut it the fuck down!

(*Aside*: Blood is not debt. I feel this way about family overall. You do not owe anyone anything because you share DNA. You have the right to remove any toxic person, even if they bore and raised and loved you. You're the one who has to live your life.)

Anyway, my relationship with my mother has nothing to do with whether I want a child of my own ("Counterpoint!"—therapist reading this), but it does stand as an example of one of the many outcomes of child-rearing. You can do everything right and if they've got the serial-killer gene, you're fucked. You can do everything right and they'll still be hurt. You can do everything right and they'll still hurt others. And there's no way you can do everything right in the first place.

So why bother?

That's my main argument now, careening toward my mid-forties. As of this writing, we're still in this goddamn pandemic—a pandemic *happened* in the first place!—and every day people are screaming about kids having access to vaccinations, whether school should be open, whether school should be closed, and I gotta tell you: I don't care! I will never have to care!

Also! The world is, unrelated to the pandemic, melting/ flooding/burning. Possibly the sky rained dead birds yesterday, maybe you fell in a sinkhole today. You definitely can't breathe that well. This planet is barely habitable now and it's only going to get worse. I'm not interested in protecting my children from that, and then dying to leave them to whatever pile of shit remains. (Also, I have no money and I own nothing. They'd end up stuck with my debts and curse my name.)

I understand *logically* why people want children: That previously mentioned imperative; it's an expression of the love you share with another person; you're from a big family and love it; perhaps you think it's just what you're supposed to do. But *in practice* it makes less and less sense to me. The world is awful. People are awful. Kids eat your money, time, attention, and will to live. (See above, re: potential outcomes.) Some parents try to hold onto some part of their pre-child coolness, but it's actually impossible, sorry.

I have not yet gotten enough out of this life, which for me has been largely miserable, to give my remaining energy and years to someone else. Maybe I'm selfish. Maybe I'm a bad woman. Maybe I'll turn forty-four and wake up desperate to conceive and it'll be too late and I'll be like one of those single celebrities who adopts in their fifties, but I truly doubt it—and anyway, if I knew the future I would just buy a lottery ticket. You'd never hear from me again.

And you'd definitely never hear my screaming baby.

FIXATIONS

VIRGOIST

In grade 11, I first heard the word "atheist" and I knew immediately it was me.

Though my grandmother would call herself a "Bible-thumping Baptist," it wasn't really true and anyway we grew up as Christmas-only Anglicans. I don't even know if or how that counts for anything. Religion was not a huge part of my life. We didn't do grace or prayers. I don't recall either of my parents speaking with any passion on the subject, but we would participate when necessary because it was the 1980s in rural Nova Scotia and no one here ever questioned why they did or believed anything. (A lot of them still don't.)

When I was in high school my aunt married a born-again Christian (a hundred red flags for that shit), stopped swearing, and started talking about the way god made her. It made me feel awkward and like I had to push my real feelings down, the way I feel now when I see old high school friends post about the lord's bounty (food they bought in a store) on Facebook.

This should be the part where I say I respect your religious beliefs and that you have a right to believe them. The second part is true, but fuck the first half—religion is the root of everything bad in the world, including the patriarchy, white supremacy, and war. Just a casual triple threat of life-ruiners. If you believe in an institution that funds and promotes these things, you do not get my respect! That's not the deal!

As I was saying, I learned this in grade 11, I don't remember where, but I do remember no one wanted to hear it. If I had to go to a church-based event I would complain afterward about the best wishes extended to me in the lord's name and my dad would say, "Oh would you *stop it.*" Independent thought? Literally, god forbid!

But here's the problem with atheism for me: I am a human on the earth and I am deep in my feelings at all times, to my own detriment, and I take constant note of coincidences and déjà vu and dreams. Because there are a lot of them. Perhaps it's because I'm an artist, but even as I do not accept that there is one god ruling all, I do believe there is more than we can see happening in front of us.

Is this idea of god something we invented so we can all ignore the futility of life and not kill ourselves en masse? Maybe! But if not to the church, that religious energy has to go somewhere. For some people it's their diet. For others it's fitness, or cars, or sports. Actors, musicians, politicians. Something to throw your most fervent energy behind without reason or logic other than you believe in it and all it stands for.

For me, that's astrology. It's a recent acquisition. For many years I believed in nothing at all and I thought I was so fucking deep, elevated above all you idiots with your little systems that were lying to you.

In 2014 I became friends with someone I'd been in quiet pursuit of for about a year. (The quiet was because she had a girlfriend. We started after she didn't, sort of. Read on.) What we actually were was what is well-known to queers as a "situationship"—more than a friendship, less than a romantic relationship, an intense and awful-for-me grey area. She was always sad, always saying one thing then doing another, and always leaving. But she was also deeply thoughtful, terrifically funny, a wonderful artist, had the best hair I've ever seen on another human (before or since), and is the only person I've ever been in love with.

She was a poet and way bought into the self-help industrial complex, a combination I was powerless against. Mary Oliver *and* Brené Brown? Good fucking luck! With her I talked about my feelings—not just for her, *all* of them—in a way I never had, digging deep into what made me, the why and how. No one had ever been this curious about what I thought. We both had imposter syndrome and bad relationships with our mothers so we bonded over that, plus movies and coffee and beer. She sent me tiny poems over Messenger and I sent her songs that reminded me of her (eventually, I would write a bunch). Conversation came easily, and constantly. *Obsessed* is not a flattering word but I would use it to describe me inside this frame.

I was always trying to define our relationship—I'd asked her on a date first; she'd politely declined and then a month later we had lunch and just never stopped hanging out—but she was in the fresh wake of a slow-motion breakup (no girlfriend, sort of!) and kept me at arm's length. She *liked* the grey area, she said, it's where she felt safe, even though I didn't. I had no choice, if I wanted to continue this relationship—and I did, more than anything I'd ever wanted before—but to wait her out. (This piece is not about that, but you can probably tell from my tone that I'm still waiting.)

That time included her moving overseas, her getting a boyfriend, then a different boyfriend, painful stretches of silence, of constant and paralyzing sorrow. (With occasional returns home in between that would make everything more complicated and always worse.)

I couldn't find the answers on earth. None of what was in front of me made any sense. Why did this person affect me so acutely? How could I be so perfectly attuned to another human who felt the same way save the one thing I needed the most? Why would that ever happen? (*Why, god, why?*) I needed a higher power to tell me it was going to be OK. Willing to do anything, to the stars I turned.

*

My birthday is September 20, 1979, and my sun, moon, and rising signs are all in Virgo. Which is very easy to tell if you know the characteristics. Here are some of them as pulled from Instagram memes:

- Attentive to detail
- Schedules + routine + order = TLA
- Keeps things inside until they come exploding out
- Loyal until fucked with
- Hates surprises and change

- Anxious overthinker
- Logical and practical
- Helpful and solution-based
- Judgmental
- Never satisfied with self
- Independent
- Uptight and prudish

All of this, times three? *Hello!*

I say all the time that I'm no fun and people often protest that declaration in support of my many feelings, but there's a difference between being *fun* and being fun*ny*. I'm the latter. I can quote *The Simpsons* or riff on a moment, but I hate the summertime and I've never done a drug in my life. You know those dating profiles that are like "I love meeting new people and I'm up for anything"? Absolutely *not*! New people are too much work—presenting some inaccurate version of yourself until you can assess them, holding back, tamping down. Up for anything??? Literally why. Most things are terrible!

When I go to the movies I have a routine, and I do not deviate from the routine. I go to the dollar store and get a bag of tiny Reese's Peanut Butter Cups and a bottle of water. Then I get a Buddy Burger at A&W. (The pandemic killed the A&W at Park Lane in Halifax, which means I now almost get murdered for a Quarter Pounder at the terrifying 24-hour Spring Garden Road McDonald's instead.) I sit in the same seat every time: On the right side, row B, behind the wheelchair row. That's because you can put your feet up and you're not pushing on anyone's seat. If the theatre is too large—I don't like to be way off to either side—I do this in the middle of the row, where there is also a bar for my feet. I go ten minutes before the posted start time and I stay for the full credits unless it's a superhero thing with ten minutes of VFX technicians. I pee before *and* after but never during.

People who come to the movies with me know the routine and they must accept it. We don't do it out of order, or at alternate places EXCEPT in case of a stat holiday, when we go to Shoppers because the dollar store is closed. (If we go to the Bayers Lake cinema we do Dairy Queen burger/Starbucks/middle of the theatre, because they're all too big.)

Nearly all of the Virgo attributes listed above apply to this and all my routines. If anyone had me tailed by a private investigator, they'd know everything within a week. I'm not saying this is a good way to live, nor do I recommend it, but as far as the stars are concerned this is why I'm like this.

*

One way astrology has changed is that the people writing it today have changed; they're not Sally Brompton's three lines in the daily newspaper talking about love being in the air or whatever. The interpreters are often queer women. Certainly, two I have come to lean on at my lowest—Chani Nicholas and Gala Mukomolova—write in a thoughtful, poetic way that considers what's going on in the world and suits my sensibilities better than Susan Miller, who's been in the game for decades and can be startlingly accurate while also being a New York society lady advising you which are the best days to get plastic surgery.

Chani and Gala—and Claire Comstock-Gay at *The Cut*, and the revolving queer astrologers at *Autostraddle*—would provide me with solace, hope, and some sort of assurance that my current state was not my fault, in meticulous, dreamy detail. It was not necessarily someone else's fault, mind you, but there would be a retrograde or a moon or a trine that would point to miscommunication, confusion, revelations, whatever I needed to hear. Chani often says, "Take what works and leave the rest" and that's the bit skeptics don't like, as if liberal interpretation of religious texts is not what's gotten us to this wretched point in the world's history.

My best friend is an Aquarius ("non-conformist attitude") and she makes hearty fun of me for this whole thing, even though we both watched her sister get married in the big Catholic church downtown to appease their mother, who, despite being a hilarious and brassy lady, is also surprisingly churchy. (My BFF herself got married in a field in rural New Hampshire.) When a tea-leaf reader talked about my cat Winston, who is big and mean and kind of violent, being a dragon in a past life—yes, I do hear myself—she said, "Oh, she saw one of Winston's hairs on your shirt" and subsequently made up this cat thing. A skeptic. It's fine, we're all skeptical of something.

But I don't know—if you're not into religion, and if you're not into astrology, what *are* you into? Everyone's had déjà vu or a too-realistic dream or an outlandish coincidence that can't be explained—what's that energy? What do you call it? God, or the stars? Luck? Nothing?

Where do you go when you need more than your people can give you? I don't know why most of us even ask for advice in the first place—we know what we're going to do, it just makes us feel better to make it seem like someone else's idea. (And all my oldest friends are straight, why would I listen to them about dating?)

Where do you turn when you don't know anything? When nothing makes sense, logic doesn't help, and hope is in short supply?

God is a concept some people just can't understand—but we can all see the stars.

COPAGANDA

Without Olivia Benson I would probably still be closeted. For a long time I didn't have cable in my apartment but we got the three Canadian networks, and CTV seemed to only ever show the various iterations of *Law & Order*. There was *L&O* original recipe, or the Mothership as it was known on Television Without Pity message boards. There was the higher-class-crimes drama *Law & Order: Criminal Intent*, starring Vincent D'Onofrio and an overflowing bucket of actorly quirks alongside the much calmer and quippier Kathryn Erbe, the Jerry Orbach of *CI*. And there was *Law & Order: Special Victims Unit*, the sex crimes show that had the curious distinction of becoming incredibly popular in its *sixth* season. (It's now in its twenty-fourth.)

I caught onto *Criminal Intent* later, Mothership never, and *SVU* out of summer boredom. It was a repeat of season 7, episode 19, which is called "Fault." Lou Diamond Phillips plays a pedophile who ends up killing a child while Benson (Mariska Hargitay) and Stabler (Christopher Meloni) are in pursuit of him, ultimately leading to a high-stakes showdown in which he's holding a gun to Stabler's head while Benson's got him at gunpoint.

Benson and Stabler have a long, incredibly emotional scene where, without explicitly saying it, he tells her he knows she has to shoot the bad guy, he knows he's gonna die, and it's OK. It's so intense that Phillips is like, "Hello, remember me?!" Anyway, a sniper takes Phillips out, and after that the partners have a different intense conversation back at the station. Benson decides she is too invested in Stabler—side note: he has a wife and many children—and needs to leave SVU. (She comes back, obviously—all of this was the offscreen set-up for Hargitay's parental leave. She won the Emmy for Best Actress that year, for this episode.)

I had zero context for any of it but I was absolutely riveted, so I went to work the next day demanding to know what Benson and Stabler's relationship was. My co-workers were like, "They're not a thing but it seems like they could be." By day's end I'd decided to watch *SVU* from the beginning so I would know for myself how we got here. (YES, I began my fandom as a Benson and Stabler shipper, how embarrassing.)

Keep in mind this was none of your fancy-pants ten-episode-season *prestige* television, this was classic network shit. That meant I had seven twenty-two–episode seasons to find (this was before Netflix or my having cable, so I torrented them all), and *then* I learned seasons four and five have twenty-five episodes each!

When *Special Victims Unit* began in 1999, Meloni was also on HBO's prison drama *Oz*. Hargitay was a movie star's daughter with a handful of credits to her famous last name, *ER* being the most notable. (I first saw her in *The Perfect Weapon*, a crappy early '90s martial arts movie, because as mentioned earlier that's what we did in my house.) It's not hard to see why *SVU* took a while to catch on—that first season looks like the Mothership, muted and grey; Benson comes off like a budget Dana Scully (herself a riff on Clarice Starling); and there are frankly way too many other cops in the squad.

As creator and executive producer, Dick Wolf's philosophy for *Law & Order* is "The story is everything"—that's why on the Mothership you rarely saw anything personal happening, didn't know who the cops were dating or what the DAs did in their spare time. It stood in stark contrast against the other police shows of the day like *NYPD Blue*, which interestingly has no cultural cachet now, and made its characters' personal flaws the bedrock of their policing styles. But as fans latched onto the typical "will they or won't they" of television couples who aren't together (everyone seems to always forget how the narrative drive disappears once the connection is finally made, and now they're just some boring people in love), and became invested in Benson and Stabler's relationship, the show itself made more room for their personal lives.

It's surely what sucked me in, but what kept me there was something totally different: subtext.

Olivia Benson, discount Dana Scully in season 1, returned the following season with her hair chopped into a short spiky do, an immense complement to her many tank tops. It was practical, it was tough, it was *gay as hell*.

Season 2 also marked the introduction of one Alexandra Cabot, the permanent district attorney. She was played by a lithe, blond actor named Stephanie March and she had incredible chemistry with Hargitay, which many viewers picked up on. Given Benson's butch presentation for the Cabot years, there was a well-developed online theory that they were (or should have been) a couple. I learned about Benson and Cabot at the same time I'd gone in on Benson and Stabler because in season 5 March had left the show: Cabot, who they thought had been murdered, was actually headed into witness protection. Olivia's tearful, anguished response, the internet decided, meant all the theories were correct. (She also happened to be there when Alex got shot and called her "sweetheart," but that's just a personal quirk of Hargitay's. Sorry y'all.)

Thus many of my current-day interests dovetailed: secret gays, a certain type of woman, and eventually, problematically, ladycops.

*

I'd always considered myself above procedural television series for the exact reason Dick Wolf considered his shows special: because they were all plot, no emotion. As someone whose main preference for any filmed entertainment is "two people in a room talking about their feelings," I thought there was nothing for me in crime-of-the-week series. I'd been pulled into *The X-Files* in high school because of Dana Scully and, it pains me to admit now, the Scully-Mulder relationship—Hollywood has made idiots out of all of us—because I certainly was not interested in bad monster makeup in foggy Vancouver. Those mythology episodes elevated it above what was, to begin with anyway, a pretty cheap sci-fi procedural.

When I got into *Law & Order* my big shows were *Gilmore Girls* and then *Friday Night Lights*, shows that were based around core characters and their relationships, eventually building out communities and worlds around them. Like a musician who doesn't write their own songs, the *Law & Order* franchise and its plot-driven emphasis didn't feel as worthy of my attention.

SVU and Olivia Benson changed that. It wasn't just the show's gay subtext—which there was not even that much of, to be honest, but we cling to the tiniest morsels—but Benson herself. Obviously, there's an incredible aesthetic appeal from the jump. She was literally born from tragedy—the product of her mother's rape—which is why she became a sex-crimes detective. She was an empathetic cop, survivor-centred, kind and gentle. She spared no perp's feelings. People hit on her all the time but she couldn't get a date to save her life, and any relationship the show deigned to show a shred of was swiftly ended by the demands of the job itself. Man after man couldn't handle her work—or, in one gross instance, was turned on by it—then disappeared like that week's rapist.

Benson set off a trend of similarly tragic lady detectives and I was obsessed with all of them. (*How* obsessed, you wonder? In 2007 I wrote a play called *Law & Order: Musical Victims Unit* and staged it at what was then known as the Atlantic Fringe Festival, and remounted it in 2012. In between, with two friends, I co-wrote an *original* cop musical called *Sirens*—also a Fringe Hit—and jumping off that production my band made an EP called *Ladycops* in 2010.)

There was Philadelphia detective Lilly Rush (Kathryn Morris) on *Cold Case*, a wisp of a blond whose mother was an alcoholic. There was Seattle detective Sarah Linden (Mireille Enos) on *The Killing*, a ghostly ginger who was abandoned by her mother and grew up in the foster care system. And there was Boston detective Jane Rizzoli (Angie Harmon) on *Rizzoli & Isles*, a snappy brunette who once escaped a serial killer. (She somehow had a great mother, played with panache by Lorraine Bracco, but her dad was absent in her adult life.)

All of these women were formed in the same image, and you can, again, find the mold in the form of Jodie Foster as Clarice Starling in *The Silence of the Lambs*: Rough upbringing, deeply intuitive, obsessive, the standout woman in a man's field.

It's probably not a mystery, then, that these shows and their sundry evidence pushed me to confront my attraction to women—I was twenty-seven (late), though some part of you always knows—and in particular, this type of woman: Ethereally beautiful (that's the kind that's typical but tinged, or in some cases soaked, with sadness) and made of great empathy, understanding and consideration of the human condition, support for the underdog, and sharp, surprising gallows humour.

I've only ever dated artists; I don't even know where I would find a lady detective in Halifax, if there are any. (There must be?) So, while the police officer portion of it is clearly not the main tenet, it would be a lie for me to say it isn't part of the appeal—as an unthreatening white lady I've always thought the police were on my side, that they kept order, and when you were in trouble who else would help you? When I was dealing with back-to-back shitty neighbours, drug-dealing men who beat women, the police always showed up when I called and never questioned my side of it. Because of course they didn't.

On May 25, 2020, George Floyd was murdered by a police officer and the Black Lives Matter movement dug in across

North America. I started hearing a word that was new to me and it gave me a sinking feeling: copaganda.

*

Copaganda—*cop* + *propaganda*—is defined as positive portrayals of law enforcement in media, from the news to the movies. Every show mentioned here is copaganda, and they aim to prove that no matter what human rights complaints you could lodge against any of the officers and lawyers depicted, their conduct is justified because they're trying to take all the bad guys off the streets. And they're fucked-up humans themselves, and *still* they are doing this selfless work!

This wasn't *news* to me, exactly, but I could dismiss it because it wasn't *just* about them being cops—it wasn't a fetish— but about how being police informed their characters, because it was the characters I actually cared about. (The characters who, to a person, were workaholics with no personal lives outside their law enforcement jobs.) And anyway, some cops were good! *These* cops were good! Not all cops!

In 2019 I wrote a feature film script called *Compulsus*, about a lesbian vigilante, Wally, who beats up abusive hipster men at night. At the same time she starts a new relationship with a woman, Lou, who turns out to be a cop. Pretty basic screenwriting thing to do—who's the worst person to be falling in love with while you're committing crimes? But then the cop decides to be in on it. Badass, right?

It felt subversive to me. In 2020 my producer and I had an application in at Telefilm, having made it through local and regional stages of approval. As the Black Lives Matter movement grew, I started getting concerned texts from friends about the script: Was I sure Lou should be a cop? What would people say? Would any actor even want to play a police officer by the time we got around to making the movie? And that word, over and over: *copaganda.*

I started asking everyone who'd read it. I asked actors I knew. Most people took a hard line: *Yes, change it. It's not worth the movie being dismissed over.* Or *No, don't. It's the highest-stakes option for your story.*

The responsibility of art, who it's for, and who it's made by, is a different essay and a continuously evolving argument anyway, so any stance I took now might be completely different by the time you read it. I do think considering communities and characterizations when you make work is important, but to expect or demand that artists only reflect their own lived experience is limiting and narrow-minded. And the ultimate result does not always reflect the amount of care an artist is investing—or where they are in their own journey. But thinking about it at all is the bare minimum, and more artists are doing that now.

It was the summer of 2020, and up until that moment in history I'd considered myself a longtime feminist who'd used my voice in media to lift up other women, a queer person, someone who used anyone's preferred pronouns, and religiously voted NDP. That was woke enough as far as I knew.

You know now that it wasn't. I turned Lou into a courthouse stenographer—still within the legal system, so she could hear the scuttlebutt and have a couple cop favours in her back pocket. A friend read the new draft and said he barely noticed the change.

Another friend made an astute observation that no one, no matter their profession, was going to be too stoked about dating a violent vigilante.

Was her being a cop worse for Wally? Sure. But it's not like *Compulsus* is an indictment of the legal system—we don't see Lou at work at all, and there was a single a-ha! moment where her job was revealed. The core plot—Wally's journey and their love story—was unaffected. I went with it.

There will always be cop stories. There will be *Law & Order*, at least in reruns, until I am dead. Procedural dramas remain the bedrock of network television; one of the most heralded shows of 2021 was HBO's *Mare of Easttown*, starring Kate Winslet as a brash, independent detective in a small town. All superheroes are cops if you think about it—as long as there are screens, Marvel will be pumping out police content.

The copaganda machine will continue to run. There's nothing I can do to stop that, but I surely no longer have to contribute to it. And Olivia Benson can forever live where she won't hurt anyone—in my heart. (And some other organs.)

LUNKS I LOVE (FOR REAL)

America has a lot of problems, and one of the biggest ones going unaddressed, in my opinion, is that there are no good male movie stars. This is partly because, as previously mentioned, the Hollywood star system has collapsed in favour of franchises. The A-list men of 1985–2010— Brad Pitt, Will Smith, and Tom Cruise—are, of course, still working, and remain big stars to an undiscerning middle America. Michael Keaton, Michael Douglas, and Kevin Costner have been largely relegated to minor comic book–movie parts. George Clooney mostly directs bland features we stopped getting excited about. They're all still kicking around.

Those franchises do need a lot of people to be in them, and most of those people happen to be generic and boring, which is just a statistics issue. Everyone can't be Florence Pugh or Gal Gadot. Four of the men in the most popular franchises are, actually, blonds named Chris. There's Evans (high school football coach), Pratt (church dork), Pine (hot dad with no kids), and Hemsworth (Australian, the best one). Each of them has a stake in the Marvel universe except for Pine, a DC guy who also led the *Star Trek* movies reboot. They're all fine; that is to say, toned and serviceable and unremarkable.

I don't go to the movies for men anyway, but it may surprise you to learn that there are a few I love, a few shining stars that rise above the porridge of superheroes and spaceships to be beacons of surprise, humour, and charm. And they're not the skinny hot-yoga man-bun types you'd probably expect me to be into considering the rest of my life. Every last one of them is a jacked-up, greased-out, core-blasting *lunk*. (Definition: A tall, brawny man, especially a sexually attractive one. Less kind definition: A stupid man.) These are my favourite lunks:

1: Zac Efron

Zac Efron is a star in the golden Hollywood–era model, a triple threat who can act, sing, and dance. Zac Efron is Fred Astaire, he's Clark Gable, he's Cary Grant. I am not kidding. First of all, he's absolutely beautiful. Second of all, he came out of the Disney television system, which is famously rigid and not geared toward, shall we say, a nuanced performance style. (See him execute a beautiful song-and-dance duet with fellow Disney alum Zendaya in *The Greatest Showman*.) Apparently he also came out of it with a drug problem, which he has recovered from, and put that energy into intense self-improvement. (Dude is *ripped*.) He's better funny than dramatic, but he can do it all. I will see any and all Zac Efron performances.

Favourite Zac movie: The comedy *Neighbors*, in which he plays the king of the frat boys at war with young parents.

2: *Adam Driver*

Driver, like Mark Ruffalo before him, comes from indie roots. And like Ruffalo after him, he pivoted into a huge studio franchise. I hate that! But I love Adam Driver, a giant ex-Navy man who was once the subject of a *New York Magazine* story about a play he was in, headlined, "How big is Adam Driver in *Burn This*?"

Driver became next-tier famous because of *Star Wars*, which I will not be addressing, but he got that part because of his seven seasons on *Girls*. Since we can't let Lena Dunham have anything, I will be the one to thank her. When he arrived in the first season, he hadn't grown into his face yet, he was just this weird topless man who very much sucked. Over the years, he became one of the show's key draws, using his physicality, bizarre (in the good way) acting choices, and theatre-honed skills to create a deep, multi-dimensional portrait of a former fuckboy. He supplements *Star Wars* and Burberry ads with weird indies and prestige studio pictures of all stripes, and even when it doesn't work (talking to you, *House of Gucci*), it's always interesting.

Favourite Adam movie: *Paterson*, the least lunkiest. A quiet Jim Jarmusch character study about a bus driver who writes poetry.

3: *Channing Tatum*

Chay Tates! His small facial features atop his large dancer's body! A juiced-up charm machine! His filmography is wildly variant: Two *Step Up*s. The Coen brothers' *Hail, Caesar!*. The Oscar bait

Foxcatcher, one of his few dips into straight drama (it works; Steve Carell's fake nose does not). I think the first *Magic Mike* is boring and overrated (Steven Soderbergh is a lot of things, but he's not fun, can relate) but the second one is a blast—self-aware, sex-positive, feminist even.

Truthfully, I had no opinion on Tatum until I saw *21 Jump Street* (2012), in which he riffed on his own lunkheaded persona to incredibly funny effect. As a trendy reboot of a 1980s cop series no one even likes, it really shouldn't have worked, but it was directed as a balls-out R-rated comedy by *Clone High* geniuses Phil Lord and Christopher Miller. The sequel, just two years later, was almost as good. That rarely happens. You just know Channing is a terrific wedding guest who leads the flash mob. He buys the whole bar a round. He'll tell you what to text a girl. He's awesome.

Favourite Channing movie: *21 Jump Street*, obvs.

4: Dwayne Johnson

There's a little-seen Florence Pugh vehicle called *Fighting with My Family* in which she plays the real-life WWE wrestler Paige. Dwayne Johnson appears as the ten-years-previous version of himself, which means he's The Rock. At this point, he had spent *years* slowly eliminating his wrestling persona from his movie-star name—Dwayne "The Rock" Johnson had become simply Dwayne Johnson—and now there was this movie where he was asking us to call him The Rock again? *Confusing*! It's the only time I've ever been upset with him.

Because Dwayne Johnson—pending potential Republican political run aside—is *wonderful*. He is a giant man, and his muscles are obviously well-trained—please read Caity Weaver's 2017 *GQ* profile and count all the cod he eats in the run of a day—but he's so charming (the smile alone!), with kind eyes and a quick wit. He won't kiss any of his lady co-stars out of respect to his wife, which sounds like something Jimmy Stewart would have done, and Dwayne Johnson is just as respected in America now as Jimmy Stewart was in the 40s. He mostly makes big loud action movies I don't like, but when he co-starred with another lunk I love, Jason Statham (see next slide), in *Hobbs & Shaw*, I slunk to it alone on opening weekend. He also co-starred with my boo Zac Efron in *Baywatch*, the 2017 film, which was very bad, but I still recommend it for Max! Lunkosity!

Favourite Dwayne movie: *The Other Guys*, a mostly forgotten comedy starring Will Ferrell and Mark Wahlberg as cops trying to emulate what they see on TV, to no avail.

5: *Jason Statham*

Statham has appeared in some of the stupidest movies of all time, including two where he must continually shock his own heart so he doesn't die, and in one of those he has sex with a lady on the track in the middle of a horse race while the crowd cheers and one of the horses jumps over them with an erection. His movies have names like *Mean Machine*, *Death Race*, and *Killer Elite*. He's been in multiple *Fast and Furious*es, four *Expendable*s, and *The Meg*, which is about a giant shark that's been hiding in an heretofore undiscovered depth of the ocean.

I love Statham for one reason and one reason only, and it is called *Spy*. It's Paul Feig's best movie, Melissa McCarthy's best movie, and Jason Statham's funniest and most self-aware performance to date. (It's the reason I knew I'd enjoy *Hobbs & Shaw*, which is part of the *Fast* cinematic universe.) McCarthy plays an undercover FBI agent out of her element, and Statham is a rogue agent who loves to go to extremes. In one scene he lists all the ridiculous things he's done—including jumping from a building with a raincoat as a parachute, putting glass shards in his own eyes, and landing a car on top of a train while he was on fire—"not the car, *I* was on fire"—that all sound like they could be real plots of his own movies. It's wonderful. Tour de force. Give him a retroactive Oscar.

Favourite Jason movie: *Spy*!

6: John Cena

The biggest curveball on the Lunk List, I think. Like Dwayne, Cena is a former wrestler, is also in the *Fast*verse, and played a version of himself in *Fighting with My Family*. He makes his share of big explodey action movies—*Bumblebee* (part of the *Transformers* franchise), *The Suicide Squad*—but unlike the rest of the guys on this list, who are fist-fighting for lead roles in tentpoles, Cena is a surprisingly gifted comedic character actor.

His best run began in 2015 with *Trainwreck*, when he played one of Amy Schumer's boyfriends ("It's like fucking an ice sculpture") who couldn't be open with her because he was likely gay. He followed that with an appearance in the Amy Poehler–Tina

Fey jam *Sisters*, as a stone-faced drug dealer to their wild middle-aged party. And his most well-rounded performance came in 2018 in Kay Cannon's *Blockers*, one of the worst names for a coming-of-age film you've ever ignored. Cena is part of a trio of parents whose daughters have made a pact to lose their virginities on prom night, and he plays against hulking type as the most sensitive, weepiest one of them all. Cena, crying, and cargo shorts: an unbeatable combination.

Favourite John movie: *Blockers*, natch.

GAY CELEBRITIES

When you're closeted, older queer people like to take swipes at you because being gay was incredibly hard for them and they're angry at you for what they see as your cowardice.

It happened to me in my early days in Halifax, which was incredibly unfair; I couldn't even admit it out loud until I was twenty-seven. Then, having learned nothing, I spent many subsequent years side-eyeing people I was sure were lying. I mean, I didn't say it to their *faces*, but behind their backs all bets were off. That guy's roommate was obviously his boyfriend, that girl keeps talking about men but *we all know better*, etc. etc. etc.

What did it fucking matter to me? IN THIS ESSAY I WILL...

There's a still-active gay journalist, now in his sixties—the key demo for closet rage—named Michelangelo Signorile, who in 1990 drove a campaign against powerful queers in Hollywood, Washington, on Wall Street, et cetera. He's considered a pioneer of outing (cool distinction), which he called "honest reporting" and only did it to public figures, because he felt their sexual orientation was as much a fact for the public record as their age or hometown.

Signorile was an editor and columnist at New York's queer alt-weekly *OutWeek* from its first issue in 1989 (its 105-edition archive is still accessible as lovingly scanned PDFs at outweek.net; Alison Bechdel, originator of the Bechdel Test, had a cartoon in the magazine). With the community deep in the age of AIDS, he used his platform to angrily call out what he saw as dangerous hypocrisy.

In June of 1990, *OutWeek*'s cover story touted, "The pros and cons of outing" and featured essays from people on either side. Signorile wrote the intro letter to the package:

"Not too long ago, some of us at *OutWeek* decided we could no longer participate in helping rich and famous gays and lesbians stay in the closet," he began. (Remember, this was a time when bisexuality was seen as bullshit, trans people were rare/ hidden, and gender identity had two options.) He goes on to disparage the term "outing"—originally referred to as "gaylisting," it was coined by "heterosexuals who had to put a quick McDonald's-like term on our behaviour"—and rails that the closet is non-existent and "arbitrary" in the first place. He goes on to express how he finds the debate "exciting, wonderful, fabulous, powerful, progressive and truly great."

Most of the featured writers were pro-outing; the magazine's arts editor, Sarah Pettit, thought focusing on the famous missed the point of all the other issues besetting the community at the time, and also made the best point: "Bigotry is not obliterated by having a witness."

This is the key tenet to my current thoughts on outing, which are sundry. My main point is that there are a lot of gay celebrities. If you come to an awards show party at my house I will gleefully—and constantly—point them out. (I will not, for obvious legal reasons, be naming them in this essay. Buy me a drink!)

Sometimes they're curiously forever single. Sometimes they're in longtime marriages—and sometimes it's one of them who's gay, sometimes it's both. Sometimes they have ex-spouses on their IMDb profiles no one can find or name. Sometimes Carrie Fisher, Hollywood royalty, who had a famous house packed full of glitzy secrets until the day she died, said it outright and no one noticed (or pretended not to).

How do I know any of these people are queer (or not)?

Well, I don't know shit. However.

It's hard to explain, but there are clear tipoffs—as famous heterosexual Winona Ryder said in *Reality Bites*, unable to define irony, "I know it when I see it!" For women they're often sexless—beautiful but exuding neither lust nor desire (stadium-level pop star, two primarily television actors from two successful series including one cult hit each, who also dated each other). Their choice of partner is similarly muted and/or has gay rumours of his own (same pop star, repeatedly), or they're never photographed/seen with anybody ever (Jodie Foster's technique for years, minus a weird period with Russell Crowe). For men it's rumours of mistreatment of sex workers (longtime movie star married three times, former movie star whose gay wife died recently), being action stars (bald man/fake name), or hailing from the UK (too many to implicate).

This is the meanest, truest one: You can't hide a gay face. You can't always tell by looking, but when you know you know.

By the way, if any famous person of any gender is repeatedly photographed or written about with a "roommate," "best friend," "gal pal," or "personal trainer"—a very good way to hide your secret love is to employ them on your team—that person is gaaaayyyyyyyyyy. This is what Signorile was railing against in the first place: folks in the closet, yes, but also the mainstream media's write-around of it. His whole deal was: why are we pretending when all the signs are there?

But his execution was reckless and shitty. Absolut Vodka ads were all the rage at the time, so Signorile created a poster series called Absolutely Queer and papered New York City with headshots of famous people from the time—Foster, Whitney Houston, Tom Selleck, John Travolta, Debra Winger—and *ABSOLUTELY QUEER* written under them in block letters. It's one thing to write about it, but to go out of your way to design a grassroots advertising campaign about it is...a bit much, no?

In a town like mine, at least, queerness is nearly as common as straightness, and I'm sick of hearing about it. Please do not guess who is the top in my presence! But outside of big cities—and I am certainly not including Halifax in that list—and odd pockets of art weirdos—that's Halifax—the average regular person is not only straight, they aren't even looking for any queers! So, Stadium-Level Pop Star or Academy Award-Winning Actor can present themselves as straight people and those people go "Cute" and get on with their fucking life.

But not me!

At literally every one of those awards show parties, and in many other social situations, my friends roll their eyes at me: "You think everyone is gay." Here's my argument: First of all, think of how many queer people you know personally, before you even open Instagram, in a Podunk town like Halifax. (Which, again, has an oddly high concentration of queer people.) Now think of how many A-list celebrity queer people there are. THERE ARE NONE. THERE HAS NEVER BEEN ONE.

Ellen DeGeneres is not A-list. Lil Nas X is not A-list. Dan Levy is not A-list, no matter how much money Netflix throws at him. Jodie Foster is no longer A-list and neither is Elliot Page (who I once ran into at the grocery store in the wake of *Juno*, and he went out of his way to tell me, a journalist, that he'd moved to LA and there was "a fellow" he was also there to be with. I remember who it was, ask me if you see me). There are no bona fide movie stars or contemporary pop stars (hi, Elton) who are out. You cannot name one, still. You can fight me about their star level, but it's never going to be A.

Because here's the thing, and this goes back to the normies: A large swath of America, which is where many, many entertainment-supporting dollars come from—hundreds of millions of people—is full of fucking homophobes. Still. And as I've said before, fame is no accident. You've gotta do a lot of shit to get it, and that includes untoward business on your way up—people are blackmailed or guilted into staying closeted by their teams or families or networks or studios. That's a lot of owed favours, to start, and then once you start amassing a team of agents, managers, assistants, accountants, merchandisers, tech crew if you're a successful musician, and on and on, well, suddenly a lot of people are depending on your gay ass for their livelihood. So if you come out, and your tour doesn't sell, then what? If you come out, and your movie tanks, then what?

In the final issue of *OutWeek*, Maer Roshan—who would go on to helm *Radar*, an incendiary blip of a pop-culture monthly—interviewed the legendary late gossip columnist Liz Smith, a target of the magazine's own outing campaign. He asked her what the effect of outing celebrities—he named Foster, a prime target of Signorile's and big star of the year because of *The Silence of the Lambs*, whose portrayal of queer people as serial killers had rankled the community—and she said something that is as true now as it was in 1991: "Her career would be ruined. There's no justice in that fact, but it's a fact nonetheless. Acting is about image. Producers are not going to cast an openly gay guy in a hot leading-man role."

(Foster didn't come out publicly for another twenty years.)

Hollywood is a business, one of the biggest. The average person cannot know of the riches contained within, but I am reasonably sure I would do whatever anyone told me for $20 million right about now. Integrity is a false god for Twitter users—stars are real people who have to live their lives, and just as I or anyone have no actual idea who they have sex with, neither can we know how many livelihoods stars are responsible for. And neither can we know what impact their upbringing, religion, and relationships have or have had on their day-to-day lives.

The reason queer people care so much about queer visibility is because it normalizes queerness. This is why we're such catty assholes about closeted people. The fact that there are so many queer actors and musicians coming up through the ranks now is legitimately amazing to me—they're starting out their careers as themselves, it's not something they're being forced to admit to after they've stopped being so famous. It's not an old rumour that's confirmed decades later in a documentary (Matt Tyrnauer's *Scotty and the Secret History of Hollywood*, 2017, total banger). It's not Britney kissing Madonna in some desperate plea for relevancy.

All change takes time, and it seems like now is theirs—celebrities can be their authentic selves immediately because of the unfamous queer elders who threw bricks at Stonewall and screamed in the streets and joined ACT UP and died in record numbers, who came before them and changed the perception of what it means to be queer. (Although, let's not get it twisted—there's a large swath of North America that still doesn't want anything other than white and straight and ideally men to remain the ideal of humanity. They're called Conservatives.)

But, among open-minded critical thinkers (and it took me a considerable chunk of years to get there myself), it's becoming more accepted as fact—as common sense—that sexuality is a spectrum, all identities are valid, and they can change at any time. But somehow entertainment, the gayest of all sectors, has been incredibly slow to change, and I do think it's because of the incredible amounts of money attached to it. It's a big old creaky business, like the government, and it takes forever for things to get shaken up out there (the number of women directing studio films in a year has still never hit double digits!).

Somebody's got to take the hit—become the first out top-tier performer, at the height of their powers—and who would volunteer for that? Who's going to put their career on the line? We forget that Ellen lost hers for years, and she was a mere sitcom actor playing a version of herself.

Someday there will be gay A-listers—I mean, the ones I'm talking about will come out in the books released after their deaths—when it's maybe not safer but they're tired of hiding. Or after someone does take the first hit. I can't expect of some random star what I don't think it's fair to demand from any old idiot, that they confirm my assumptions. Like waiting for that longtime crush to figure herself out, you have to be patient and frustrated.

But until then, we look and we speculate, and we gossip.

THE PERFECT MOVIE RUNTIME
IS 90 MINUTES

With no apologies to Martin Scorsese, the Marvel Cinematic Universe, or Peter Jackson: the perfect movie runtime is 90 minutes.

If your movie runtime starts with a 1, you have fucked up. If it starts with a 2, everyone hates you.

Sure, sure there's *The Decalogue* and *La Flor* and *The Godfather* and any number of international endurance cinema productions (looking at you, *Drive My Car*), but disrespectfully, fuck all that. We are awash in content and our attention spans are ruined. If you can't tell a story in 90 minutes, film is the wrong format for that story. Write a novel. Make a record or a television series. Theatre, too, is a visual medium if that's what's important to you.

You don't have to leave to pee in a 90-minute movie. The sun is still up when you come out of a matinee. It makes a double feature much easier to digest (and still shorter than *The Irishman*). It doesn't have to be the only thing you do that night.

If you subscribe to the three-act structure—no one's saying you have to!—a 90-minute script divides up beautifully (one screenplay page equals, unless you're Amy Sherman-Palladino or Kevin Smith, one minute of screen time): Act I (thirty pages), Act II (thirty pages), Act III (thirty pages).

Thorney's perfect 90-minute movie list:

Before Sunset (80 minutes)
The Breakfast Club (97 minutes)
Frances Ha (86 minutes)
Gravity (91 minutes)
Lady Bird (94 minutes)
Medicine For Melancholy (88 minutes)
Once (86 minutes)
Pretty in Pink (96 minutes)
Stand By Me (89 minutes)
Toy Story (81 minutes)

Consider this from a production perspective: As of publishing, the films of the Marvel Cinematic Universe combined cross two full days into a third, in terms of watch hours. They're all two hours minimum; a *shameful* number of them knock on two-and-a-half hours; *Avengers: Endgame* has the gall to hit three. They cost hundreds of millions of dollars to produce—the average is $200 million, and to date Marvel has spent over $4 billion on these things. (This is just production btw, not advertising or merchandising.)

Do you know what cuts money from the budget? CUTTING SCRIPT PAGES! Make the movie shorter and everyone wins: The movie costs less to produce so you'll make more money, it's kinder to an audience already prone to repeat theatrical viewings—speaking of which, you can jam more screenings into a day—and maybe those third-act incomprehensible CGI fights will be eliminated because not one is necessary, narratively helpful, or competently rendered.

Now clearly, spending money makes money in the MCU's case, but *why*? Why overspend on a long-ass movie when you could spend moderately on a shorter script and make *more*? There is not one superhero movie that doesn't need to be 20 minutes shorter. *Not one!* Even the ones I like (*Captain Marvel*, the *Thor*s) all devolve into the same final battle where I don't know what the fuck is going on. We all know going in the hero's going to win (except in the rare case that someone dies, and we always know that in advance too—*did you even read the comics?!*), so make it lean and interesting! Make it *practical*, perhaps? Switch it up! Save a dollar or 10 million!

In 90 minutes, you could:
- Fall in, or out, or out then back in/of love
- Come of age
- Do a heist
- Perform a musical
- Come home from space
- Save Christmas

That's a lot of story options. No need to gum it up with ten plotlines, three action set pieces, and five epilogues.

The perfect movie runtime is 90 minutes. It just is.

CARTOONS

As of this writing in the year of our lord two thousand and twenty-one, I am forty-two years old and I watch at least three episodes of cartoons a day: Two *Bob's Burgers* and a *Simpsons*. And sometimes a *King of the Hill*. (Occasionally, shamefully, a Seth MacFarlane production slips in when there are no other options.)

I watch these cartoons on cable television, which I pay for. My combined internet and cable bill is $189 a month. That's *basic* cable, by the way, sixty channels total, of which I watch about five, and almost all are for reruns of cartoons.

The Simpsons arrived in 1989. It's laughable to think about now but Bart Simpson, with his anti-achievement stance, was considered controversial. *The Cosby Show* was the reigning pop-culture king, and its portrayal of a kind-hearted family—oh, how we would come to reframe this entire deal—led by one of the most respected men in America (cough) had set the tone for a gentler television. The crude *Simpsons*—and the show looked legitimately awful for years, but we're talking content too—was a stark contrast to the jazz-tinged, gentrified New York–based adventures of the Huxtables. And it was a huge hit.

In 1989 I was in grade 6 and *Simpsons* merch was all the rage. Even more than thirty years later I have a distinct memory of my teacher saying, "I just don't think you should be proud to be an underachiever" and banning shirts with negative sayings on them ("Don't have a cow, man" was also offensive to her). So I had this shitty white sweatshirt with a printed picture of the Simpson family, saying nothing, on it. I did and still do think 2D Simpsons make no sense.

A lot of us who were adolescents in that time were probably attracted to the show not just because it was a brand-new animation style—most of us knew the sleek and beautiful line drawings of Disney and Saturday morning cartoons; this was bedraggled and scrappy and very, very yellow—but because it pissed off our parents. (No wonder that was the Me Generation, with "problems" like a mildly offensive 22-minute television program.) We were drawn to what was forbidden. If you were me then, you stayed for three decades. If you're me now, you're still there.

But *why*? Perhaps I have an overly kind view of myself—not usually!—but I don't consider myself "one of them," the typical *Simpsons* nerd who's also into comics and Marvel movies and video games. (By "one of them," I mean men.) If I knew a man my age who watched as many cartoons as I do I would consider his emotional growth stunted and I would make fun of him directly to his doubtlessly suffering wife. It's not something I'm proud of, even as certain cartoons—*BoJack Horseman, Tuca & Bertie*—are credited with their insightful depictions of the human condition. There are the smart, saucy ones like *Archer* and *Big Mouth* that are okay to like. There are the Marvel and

Star Wars ones I don't and will never care about. There's anime, an art form I know nothing about.

But these nuclear-family cartoons—*The Simpsons, Bob's Burgers, King of the Hill*—I have watched over and over for literally decades. Obviously, they're sharp and funny and quotable; you know all the memes. *The Simpsons,* specifically, is its own language and only a select few have kept up with their studies. Only fellow over-forties know the random references—outside of the Homer-disappearing-into-bushes gif, "Everything's coming up Milhouse," and the recent and very late addition, "Don't make me tap the sign"—that are sparked by a joke, or a comment, or literally anything at all happening.

During the first year of the pandemic I dug deep into comfort entertainment—teen movies, *The Office,* John Mulaney specials. That made sense to me. The world didn't, so I sunk into things I was familiar with, that I could count on being funny and emotional.

Cartoons fill that need for me year-round, because of the following elements.

1: Animation

Am I an animation freak? No. I like these shows and I like Pixar, but I don't consider myself an aficionado of any kind, nor do I seek it out. I'd say I'm more likely to watch an animated show than I am an animated movie, even if I don't ultimately care about that show. (I've watched all of Matt Groening's *Disenchantment,* and have no memory of it other than Abbi Jacobson's name is Bean.)

I'm also not a special-effects and/or fantasy person. If a movie is made by a team of computer specialists, I do not care. If actors were forced to perform next to green foam on a stick, I feel bad for them. If there's a dragon, no. But the three shows I love are based in reality, real humans in real places, even if the characters never age. Outlandish things certainly happen—*Bob's* has a musical number most episodes!—and due to the format they're able to jump around in time, introduce random characters for a week, and just basically bend the laws of science if need be. That's the sweet spot of fantasy for me. Real life, but heightened. Everything goes back to the way it was at the end of the episode. Familiar.

2: Humour

Some of the best jokes—construction, timing, delivery—live in animation. And because we're not actually watching real people, they can be as mean or otherworldly as they want, cause we're resetting next week. Some of my favourite episodes of *The Simpsons* contain more laughs than silence. The single best episode of *King of the Hill* can be summed up in three words: "That's my purse!" And *Bob's Burgers*, which even though it's more than a decade old still counts as "the new one" to me, has a humour rate easily on par with *The Simpsons* (and way more song and dance). It's the jokes that up the rewatchability factor as well.

3: Guest stars

There's an episode of *King of the Hill* called "A Beer Can Named Desire" (season 4, episode 6) where the Hills visit New Orleans for a football game and Bill goes with them because he has family there. That family is voiced by all three of The Chicks—who play randy sisters, cousins of Bill's—and Meryl Fucking Streep as their mother. There's no movie or live-action television show that could ever exist in which this would happen in any effective way. But in animation it's a stone-cold classic. To be a guest star on *The Simpsons* is a rite of passage—my favourite is Ron Howard, for my money a better vocal actor than film director—and now so is singing a song on *Bob's*.

4: Emotion

None of this would matter if these characters didn't have relationships, personalities, and real feelings. People stick with these shows because they're good-hearted and empathetic, no matter how many unrealistic things have happened in the episode. It always comes back to love and family. And because there are no actual human faces, you can project what you need onto the animation, and get what you want in response.

So, I'm a grown person who watches cartoons. A lot. Repeatedly. Perhaps I should be putting my cable money toward therapy, but in a much more entertaining way, aren't I already doing that?

RANTS
&
RIFFS

AIR CONDITIONER CULTURE

One of the best-known and least-appealing tenets of my personality is that I hate the summertime. That's always been true, even as I spent much of my adolescence outside, and Saturday mornings at softball games. I don't know if, as an adult, it's simply a contrarian reaction to my rural upbringing—this far into the book, you know how much is—but I do enjoy the outdoors as a gathering place. I walk everywhere as long as the weather is good, but bad weather to me includes sunny days above 25 degrees, and really that is pushing it.

I am not immune to the gauzy nostalgia of summer: the laziness, the anything goes-ness, the smell of burning charcoal, the idea that days are numberless and nameless and endless. It's a holdover for grown-ass people from school days.

Once, in 2012, I even wrote a love letter to summer in *The Coast*, and it contains this psychotic paragraph (I have not owned a bike since I was eighteen):

No other time of year makes you look back with dusk-lit longing at nights, loves, fires and drinks gone by with such an acute sense of nostalgia, either. Late summer of

2010, jammed full of a hurricane, a heat wave and a rash
of swarmings? All we remember now is the communal
meal we had in the dark that night, the 2am bike rides
to Video Difference and the cool morning air coming
through the window before the world heated up again.

Okay, Thorney!!!

Overall, I spend the weeks from June to Labour Day largely enraged. People are drunk constantly, screaming in their yards at night, setting off fireworks at 2:00 A.M. for no discernable reason, staggering through the streets in large, horny groups and generally being loud, irresponsible, and annoying.

Add to that how you can't sleep, how it's too hot to clean or make food or fold laundry, how many people attempt to mask their sweat with colognes and perfumes, how you can't walk anywhere without bringing a second shirt, how mad your pets are, and the inevitable closure of all bodies of water due to bacteria. (Side note: lakes are disgusting!) Summer, he's the worst. (There's no way summer, imposing and inescapable, is not a man.)

There's an old joke about Nova Scotia: "If you don't like the weather, wait five minutes and it'll change." Oh, how we coasted on that for decades! It's even more true now, but it's because of climate change, and nobody laughs.

The truth is we never got much of a summer for a long time. Just sort of middling low-20s days, sometimes rain, sometimes not, a week or two of hot and hey, here was autumn coming to kick out the mugginess.

(Now autumn is a whole different story. If there was a place on the earth that was autumnal year-round I would live and die there, even if the only industry was coal mining. I would murder anyone autumn asked me to. I'd leave my wife for her. I don't have a wife but I would get one and divorce her just so autumn would know the depths of my devotion. She is a poem, a show tune, the best movie you've ever seen. She's the only good season and we all know it.)

In 2018 I was working in a place with no air conditioning. In fact, in my nineteen years at *The Coast* we were in three different offices, and none of them ever had central air, because the boss doesn't like A/C. And not only that, but she would open all the windows and fling the door wide to let all the hot fucking air in.

Now to be briefly fair to *Coast* management, the problem here is not ultimately their personal preference but the fact that in Nova Scotia there has never been—and still isn't, even as we boil alive—a culture of air conditioning. Cities like Toronto and New York are prepared for summer with the classic in-window A/C clunker. When I went to Texas in June of 2015, I marvelled at both the average daily temperature of 34 and how every building, including our rented apartment, was humming with A/C. Shop doors would be wide open and an icy breeze would blast you as you passed. (The root of America's energy crisis becomes very obvious once you're in it.)

But Nova Scotia simply wasn't ever consistently hot enough to justify it. I am a reasonable, sweaty person, and I get that.

In 2018, however, summer was fully unlivable. It was 40 degrees for a month straight, and that is not an exaggeration—look it up. I remember this because I cried often while looking at my weather app. I'd go to the movies, my one respite, but they'd put signs up saying their air conditioning was malfunctioning in the humidity and watch out because the floors were slippery. I didn't have A/C in my second-floor apartment, or any apartment ever, either, so every day was an absolute fucking slog. No relief at the office, no relief at home.

At work I had a fan—paid for out of my own pocket, of course; management bought one jumbo box of Freezies, once—and planted it on my desk directly in front of my face. But it was too loud for phone interviews, which were frequent, so I had to turn it off constantly because my desk was pushed up against another desk and my chair backed onto another chair. We were journalists, so we were on the phone a lot.

Everyone was surly. No one was well-fed because it was too hot to cook. We couldn't sleep. Many of us had heat rashes. We couldn't even do our work because people weren't answering their phones or emails from the beach. It was cranky and uncomfortable and awful.

And because the door was constantly propped wide open, it meant neighbourhood weirdos could wander in and out unimpeded. People often used the office as Google, asking for directions, which is fine. The big requests were for plastic bags (?) or to use the phone. And because we were a newspaper, people often dropped by to express their anger or dismay. Sometimes it was misguided—they'd mistaken us for the *Chronicle Herald*, which was housed in a huge glass building nearly four kilometres from our tiny hole in the wall—and sometimes it was specific.

One 40-degree-ass day in August a woman strolled into the office and started yelling at my A/C-hating boss, who happened to be perched up front. There had been a mass shooting in New Brunswick the day before, the same day the paper came out, and we'd coincidentally printed a screed that made light of shooting someone in the face or some such. (*The Coast* has a very popular section called "Love The Way We Bitch" wherein people can send anonymous rants of all stripes.)

This lady was mad at our tastelessness, even though the timing was not our fault—the paper had clearly gone to press before the shooting. And this particular boss was never great at dealing with the public because she had no capacity to apologize, so the woman was frustrated with her non-response.

And then the woman said, "What if somebody came here and shot all the journalists?"

Reminder: This was Trump times, "fake news" times, and a huge anti-media sentiment had set in across the US and eventually with the parroting Conservatives in Canada.

Our office was a crammed open-concept so we were all sweatily sitting there and we all heard it. Most of us fell silent; somebody yelled, "What the fuck?"

Then, because the door was being held open for her by a rock, the woman—who, to her credit, I guess, seemed to realize instantly that she'd gone too far—disappeared into the blaze of the day.

Do you see how air conditioning would have prevented all of this?

The door would have been closed, and a barrier of any kind is all most people need to stop their outrage in its tracks. Odds are that person was just walking by and happened across the office by accident, and we made it easy for her to storm in and imply we should be murdered.

As I write this before noon on a late August weekday in 2021, the humidex in downtown Halifax is at 37 degrees Celsius (a debate for another time—if it "feels like" a temperature, is that not the temperature? One of the rare times I say *fuck science*). We've always had an annual hurricane scare here, and the last one infamously collapsed a crane on top of a downtown building, but the day-to-day weather has changed so much—it'll be 30 degrees and sunny, then the sky will turn black and an absolute torrent will knock out power, only to return to the original forecast like it never happened. My sister in Colchester County got womped by a *tornado* in July. What used to be noteworthy has become commonplace.

Including heat waves.

Here's the part that infuriates me: All the science points to global warming. We're in a full-on climate crisis. Yet still we suffer through it! You can go to the movies (sometimes) or the mall, but otherwise you're on your own. Go to someone's house and *maybe* they have a heat pump—which acts as a dehumidifier and air conditioner in hot temperatures—but largely you're just sweating your way around town, drunk in backyards and waiting for night to come. Two summers ago in a fit of humid anger I bought a stand-up A/C unit, but my ceilings are so high it's largely ineffective, and very very loud. My TV is normally on 11 and I have to push it to 50 to reasonably hear it. My cats are at risk of depression because I keep the windows shut and blinds down until 7:00 P.M. (on a good day).

We would never expect anyone to suffer through the winter with no heat. Coldness, too, is a human right! (And yes, increasing air conditioning will just kill the earth faster, but it's trying to kill us now—who do you suggest should win?) Cold kills more people than heat does, but in 2003 a heat wave took out ten thousand elderly French people. Nova Scotia's core population is old as hell! You think that won't happen here?!

Normalize cold, it's already too late.

CRAZY DOG LADY

Put this book down for a sec and give "crazy cat lady" a Goog. When I did it, I got 381 MILLION results. Along the top of the page was a row of images of Eleanor Abernathy, an all-timer tertiary *Simpsons* character colloquially known as, of course, The Crazy Cat Lady.

She first appears in the excellent season 9 episode "Girly Edition," in which Lisa and Bart co-host a news show for Springfield Elementary. When Lisa's serious reportage is outshone by Bart's mawkish human-interest stories, she tries to find her own, and ends up at Eleanor's tiny house with its unmown front lawn. She parks a camera in the driveway and points it at herself.

"They call her The Cat Lady," begins Lisa's intro. "People say she's crazy just because she has a few dozen cats. But can anyone who loves animals that much really be crazy?"

The house's door opens and Eleanor appears, bellowing gibberish in a pink nightdress, purple cardigan, and one wonky eye. Then she charges at Lisa, literally throwing cats at an eight-year-old.

Cut to some train tracks. "The old Union Pacific doesn't come by here much anymore," Lisa intones dramatically. Cue ten seconds of train ripping by, UNION PACIFIC flashing past repeatedly. In classic *Simpsons* form, you think that's the joke, but there's one more level: When the train is gone, there's The Cat Lady, who heaves another armful of felines at a child.

I'm calling her Eleanor, but the show didn't even give her a real name until nearly a decade later, in season 18, when we learn that she's a double Ivy League grad who used to be a lawyer *and* a doctor. Overworked, she started drinking, then hoarding cats. We know the rest—we met it first.

Eleanor Abernathy is based on Big Edie Beale, the cousin of Jackie Kennedy famously depicted in the documentary *Grey Gardens*, living in a dilapidated mansion with her sister and many cats. At one point in the film, they're so poor they literally eat cat food.

The hoarding of cats is a legitimate form of obsessive-compulsive disorder; if I had to theorize why it's connected to women most often, I'd guess it's because the world at large likes to think everything is a stand-in for a baby.

But you don't need more than a single cat to be called a cat lady, with all its implications. When I posted my CBC-career-ending tweet about the premier's son (turn to page 180), my avatar was that of my cat Steve, who I plucked out of a barn as a kitten, lived with for nineteen years, and who had died the year before. When someone who was clearly the premier's son's friend attacked, he made sure to call me a cat lady in the process. Because we know what it implies: lonely, sexless, pathetic loser.

Obviously, this is not true. First of all, losers come in all forms of pet ownership. Secondly, everyone cool has a cat. Thirdly, if you work in the arts and live in apartments as is the case in my peer group in Halifax, you're largely not allowed to have a dog scooting around on anyone's precious hardwood floors. If you want something soft to hug, it's gotta be a cat.

I have another equally weightless, fully anecdotal theory to entrench in your precious pop culture: The "crazy" women don't love cats.

They love dogs.

*

For the record I too love dogs, I just don't want a baby. (Also see above re: rented hardwood floors.) One of the only good men I've ever known was a Nova Scotia Duck Tolling Retriever named Jack. For the past decade, I've watched many of the women around me acquire dogs as pets.

And not just any dog: They're often a fancy breed from out of the country and can fit comfortably in a small duffel. Various terriers. Long-haired chihuahuas. Pugs. Dogs with "Toy" in their given scientific names.

I'm not saying there's a particular person who has a small dog and a particular person who has a large dog, but the large-dog people do not put capes on their pets and take them to a beer garden. They don't drag them to parties and sit with them on their laps. They don't put them in a glorified purse and take them on public transit.

Then there is social media. I used to have a feature called Steve of the Day—I took a picture of my cat every day and posted it on Instagram! I'm not unlike you! BUT.

I did not start an account, @SteveThorne, and post in the first person, in Steve's voice. You did for your dog, though!

*

In the spring and summer of 2021, deep into the pandemic, the city of Halifax was ensnared in two monumentally ridiculous debates: One was about whether bars should be allowed to sell to-go cocktails along with takeout. (I love alcohol as much as I love cats but I cannot imagine considering this a problem in my or anyone's life. By the way, they won, mere minutes before restrictions were lifted and people were allowed to eat in restaurants again. Great job, everyone. Just go to the liquor store!) The other was whether dogs should be allowed on patios. You can probably guess my thoughts from the beer garden bit above, but I shall expound—your dog does not want to "hang out" with you by lying under a table for three hours! Your dog does not want to look at other dogs while being this bored! Your dog does not care about your online engagement!

Even though most of the beer gardens and some patios allowed it, until 2021 dogs on patios were technically banned in Halifax, unless they were service dogs, for food safety reasons. The entitled, never-satisfied local restaurant business community was of course fighting to change it—the feeling being if people could bring their dogs, they would stay longer and spend more money.

DO YOU REALIZE HOW FUCKED UP THAT IS?

That's how co-dependent you people are: Businesses discovered they could make enough money off you to make it worth fighting the provincial government for! And *they won*! Who's lonely and pathetic now?

There are also the rescue-dog people, who have their dogs flown in from developing countries as part of various international programs. More than once I've seen people asking for rides to neighbouring provinces to pick up a dog, or posting to ask if they knew anyone who was traveling to the Dominican Republic and could bring a dog home.

In my experience, the rescue-dog people feed their animals a better diet than they themselves personally eat, probably to make up for the doubtless awful circumstances the dogs lived through before now. As someone who has been roped into the racket that is vet food, I understand that we want better for our pets than the grocery store trash made of who knows what. But I hate going to the grocery store and cooking for *myself*, I'm not also making my pets full-on meals. I literally cannot afford to feed a family of three; it's one of the many reasons I don't have children.

They buy and clothe their dogs in coats and vests and boots, because often rescues come from warm climates and have never seen winter. Is it necessary? I've never asked, but come on.

Ideally, we'd be eliminating all stereotypes that include the pejorative term "crazy," which has slowly but surely and rightfully become a word we don't say anymore, but if you must dismiss a woman as lonely and sad: from now on, at least give her a dog.

FUCK SPACE

I am not a whimsical person. I don't like fantastical things. I can't believe in god.

If you wanna settle in for a good meteor shower, if you wanna try to take a good photo of the moon on your phone (impossible), if you wanna drive to the ocean and marvel at the stars, I'm down for all of that.

But in general, in practice, and overall: fuck space.

I used to have this bit where I theorized that every man is gay, because all men do is try to best one another—the most money, the youngest/hottest wife, the fastest car, the biggest whatever the fuck—and only other men care about these things, so clearly they all want to bang each other. (This bit invariably makes straight men very defensive.)

The lives lost, money spent, and time wasted just for personkind to attempt to ruin other parts of the universe, when we can't even get earth right, is astounding to me. The US has given NASA over $650 billion since 1915. The twenty-year "space race" between the US and Russia was peak dick-swinging—peak sexual tension if you will—involving SEVEN American presidents, and for WHAT. There's no escape! We're living in the mess we made and there's no way out! Maybe for a couple rich guys, but when there's no one left down here to tweet about them they'll just careen their spaceships straight into the sun.

Canada is rarely involved in intraterrestrial conversations except for three times:

- The invention of the Canadarm, officially delivered to NASA in 1981.
- In 1992, Dr. Roberta Bondar became the first Canadian woman in space.
- And in 2013, Sarnia's own Ned Flanders, Chris Hadfield, became an international star for tweeting pictures of space and singing "Space Oddity," one of the hackiest songs one could perform, at campfire level, from the International Space Station.

People get incredibly mad at me for slagging Hadfield because he was sharing his unique perspective, but I think you're all distracted by his mustache. Let me tell you a story, and I should preface this by saying I was already not a fan going in.

In September of 2013, I was in the audience for the premiere screening of *Gravity* at the Toronto International Film Festival, held at the Princess of Wales Theatre downtown (capacity: two thousand). *Gravity* stars Sandra Bullock as a woman stranded in space. Directed by Alfonso Cuarón, it's essentially a series of disasters, gripping and nail-biting even on repeat viewings, even when you know how it turns out. It's terrific.

If you've never been to a big film festival premiere, here's the vibe: It's a mix of very famous people, very important people, regular Torontonians who have paid $50 and stood in line all day, and random doinks like me (visiting press). A real clash of the classes. There are always speeches—depending on the film it could be any number of festival reps and sponsors, but there's always a programmer, and if the director and cast are on hand, they'll be introduced. It adds a good twenty minutes to every screening.

At this one, the programmer had introduced Cuarón and Bullock, and made a couple notes. One was that Roberta Bondar—again, THE FIRST CANADIAN WOMAN IN SPACE—was in the room. Some people hadn't heard that name since the '90s, some not at all, but there was polite Canadian applause. I looked back from my second-row seat—a terrible choice on my part, the movie was screening in 3D—to see Bondar standing and waving from the back of the theatre.

Then the programmer introduced another space person, fresh off his viral nerd tour, and it was Hadfield. He was about eight rows behind me, in a tux. He stood and waved too, and the difference between him and Bondar, actual achiever of yesteryear, was the crowd went wild for him.

At the Q&A afterward—for a movie this man had *nothing to do with* other than *he actually went to space* which *no one in the movie did or has done*, might as well interview me about my 9/11 experience because I watched CNN that day—some idiot in the audience asked Hadfield (?!?!) how the film compared to his time in space.

Hadfield: "It would have been a lot more interesting if Sandy was there."

Bullock: Smiling gamely, clearly thinking, "*Who* the *fuck* is this person?"

Thorney: [rage blackout]

I'm sorry sir, but the *nerve* of you to pull focus from Academy Award Winner Sandra Bullock, here kicking off her awards season campaign for a beautiful movie she made without ever hearing your name?! What gives you the right to call her *Sandy*? How dare you hit on her?!!!

Later, he started a band. Unforgivable.

My space hatred, by the way, extends to space movies, and there are so many, and all my best girls keep going there. There's Bullock; Jodie Foster as a scientist in *Contact* and a bad guy in *Elysium*; and Jessica Chastain and Anne Hathaway in *Interstellar*—a laughably bad movie I once got in a fight with someone over at a Christmas party (Murph!!!). I do not care about *Star Wars*, *Star Trek*, any of the Marvel ones that involve space, the *Alien* franchise, or any miniseries co-produced by Tom Hanks and Steven Spielberg.

Occasionally one breaks through—*Arrival*, because it was beautiful; *The Martian*, because it was funny—but largely I do not and will not bother. As someone who now makes movies, to me you might as well fund an actual trip to space if you're going to finance a movie about space. It's gotta be around the same budget.

The universe is objectively amazing; I'm not fully lacking in awe. But can we not leave well enough alone? Can we not let the goddamn universe exist without us spending billions of dollars going up there to look fruitlessly for shit to save us? Can we not save that money and put it into solutions literally on the ground? Clean water, maybe? Not gonna find that in space!

Can we not gaze up at the stars, wistfully sigh, "I wonder," and have that be enough?

Fuck space.

THAT WORD, IT DOES NOT MEAN
WHAT YOU THINK IT MEANS

As a recovering journalist, triple Virgo, pedant, and all-around unfun person, the active misuse and/or misspelling of words (and punctuation!) makes me want to take an iconic leap into the curated sea.

Please do not yell at me about dyslexia and other learning disorders: *I know*. I am not talking to those people, or people who struggle and do try and just can't grasp certain rules. I am talking to lazy and/or trendy people who just don't bother and think it's fine (a large, large swath of the internet, then).

Please also do not yell at me about how it's discriminatory or ableist or snooty to expect people to spell things, or use apostrophes, correctly. I am extremely online and I understand vernacular and slang, and how language evolves with or without us. (I absolutely struggled with "they" as a singular pronoun when it became common and now I don't! People grow!)

It doesn't mean you get to be *wrong*. Fuck that, and fuck you.

Here is a list of the worst of the worst, in my opinion.

1: Iconic

This is the worst offender I can think of in my entire time as a human with a working brain on the planet Earth. The etymology of it is a mystery to me, and a different book, but using "iconic" with the same frequency as we would normally deploy "cool" had already seeped into life when I was leaving *The Coast* in 2019 because I have a distinct memory of screaming at my co-workers about it. It's been years for sure. ("How long have we been on this rock?" –Willem Dafoe in *The Lighthouse*, and me right now.)

The definition of *iconic*, via Merriam-Webster (dot com, know your audience) is "of, relating to, or having the characteristics of an icon; widely recognized and well-established; widely known and acknowledged especially for distinctive excellence."

So whatever you're calling "iconic," BY DEFINITION, should have the cultural impact, talent, and longevity of MADONNA.

Here are some of the things Twitter called "iconic" on the day I wrote this:

- BTS
- A picture of Harry Styles wearing a shirt that says HOT N HARD
- Ariana Grande tweeting "thank u, next" in 2018
- A bangle bracelet designed by Michael Kors
- The song "Fancy" by Twice
- A cake made of peanut butter and Snickers bars
- The brownstone from *Breakfast at Tiffany's*
- Jimmy Vesey being signed to the New Jersey Devils
- Sonic the Hedgehog

- The poster for *Scream 5*
- Tim Curry's command of the screen in *The Rocky Horror Picture Show*
- Cardi B

Do any of these things sound Madonna to you? (Maybe Tim Curry.)

2: Curated

Curated means picked by a professional. You can only curate art and museum exhibitions, so excuse me but what the fuck are you talking about with your "curated" playlist, wedding theme, or Instagram feed? Of course you picked it! Who else would? You think you're being fancy but you're just being a know-nothing dickhead. There is nothing special about the thing you curated, unless you're Madonna. Then you've curated something iconic. Otherwise, you just made a list.

3: Bespoke

Bespoke means custom. That's the beginning and goddamn end of it. To call something specifically designed for a specific reason "bespoke" is not wrong, but it *is* douchey.

4: Egregious Apostrophes

The apostrophe represents the character(s) that has/have been removed to create the contraction. "It is" becomes "it's," "has not" becomes "hasn't," "we are" becomes "we're." Some language rules are tricky but this one is not.

There used to be an excellent mid-range restaurant in Halifax called Rogues Roost and between the sign, the menu, the website, and the logo on the beer glasses, it was either Rogues (where all the rogues), Rogues' (where a group of rogues), or Rogue's (where a single rogue) Roost(s). One time I got so fed up I called them in a journalistic capacity to ask which one it was and *they did not know.* That restaurant is now a Lululemon.

I will not even go into a restaurant if it's got a sandwich board with bad spelling and erroneous apostrophes. Attention to detail is important—if you're writing "Tonight's Special's" as your front-facing marketing tool, what is going on in the kitchen?

5: A Brief List Of Things People Have Been Writing Or Saying Wrong My Whole Life

- It's Interac, not Interact
- It's sherbet, not sherbert (There's not and has never been a second R!!!!)
- It's chaise longue, not chaise lounge (yes, you lounge in it)
- It's PIN/SIN not PIN/SIN number (the N stands for number)
- "$5 million" is five million dollars, "$5 million dollars" is five million dollars dollars
- It's restaurateur not restauranter

6: Semi-Colons

You don't know how to use them. You just don't.

SIDEWALK CLOSED USE OTHER SIDE

Nothing in the city of Halifax—not the transit system, the housing market, the liquor laws, or how we can't have anything nice—infuriates me on a *daily* fucking basis like construction.

Halifax is obsessed with being seen as a "world-class" city, which is laughable in a town whose official food is the donair and unofficial clothing line is clipart of an anchor. It's why they built a new convention centre, and why every sports-related building is approved—tourism, baby! Never mind that we've been pushing the same outdated shit for decades—fiddles, fish, the sea, shoot me.

Whenever anyone asks me what my dream job is, my answer is always to go back in time and be born the child of a Halifax developer. They are allowed to do fucking *anything* in this city, it's astonishing. And this is not some knee-jerk leftist reaction to progress or gentrification—I am a direct beneficiary of gentrification—it's a resistance to giving some sleazebag permission to block out the fucking sun like Mr. Burns.

New condos drive up rents, which does not affect me personally because my landlords are my friends (although if we have a falling out I shall be relocating to my forever backup plan, the ocean), and it's not like I need parking or am in favour of abandoned buildings so what is my problem?

My problem is that Halifax has a giant city council with a huge urban/rural divide. The majority of HRM city councillors live outside of the downtown core and drive everywhere and have their own parking spot, and they happily approve every giant building that's put in front of them, because PROGRESS! PEOPLE! TAX DOLLARS! TORONTONIANS!!!

My problem is the sidewalks.

My problem is walking.

When "world-class" cities like New York or the worldliest classiest Canadian city, Vancouver, erect new buildings, they build temporary sidewalks for the duration of the construction. They fit the construction into the busy daily life of their cities.

Halifax? Oh, Halifax has a single trick up its dingy little flannel sleeve:

SIDEWALK CLOSED

USE OTHER SIDE

The number of times I flip off this sign in the run of an average day is immeasurable. I have drunkenly kicked them over. I have gotten in fights with random idiots who put one up on a corner so they can paint their house a full block away and not have to worry about dropping shit on people. (These people are not the police. Anyone can get one of those signs and put them wherever they want. They have zero authority over anything. If one of them yells at you, tell them Thorney said go fuck yourself.)

Not only do they not do the temporary sidewalk here—
which is 100 percent in the city bylaws, oops I guess someone
forgot to enforce it!—they have also taken to building a cement
wall halfway into the road, eating up a full lane of traffic, so the
lazy assholes in their trucks can conveniently drive in and out of
the work site. I hate these walls with my life. There is one two
blocks from my house that has been up for three years, and last
summer one went up *across the street on the same block*. That
means to legally walk to the theatre at the bottom of that street, I
have to cross the street three times in one tiny stretch. The walls
cause sightline issues, there is no traffic light of any kind, and
people can't drive in this town. Sites that close together should
be illegal.

But when you're a developer and you've got millions that
you attained somehow—nefariously? Who's to say!—and you're
also greasing *some*body's hand to use the city and the police
force to push the homeless people out of high-visibility areas,
who the fuck is going to stop you from building a wall in the
middle of traffic for years at a time? Who's going to stop you
from full-on blocking a *traffic light* at the corner of Gottingen
and Cogswell? (*Those* developers actually *built* a temporary sidewalk (good!) then promptly hauled a concrete block across its
entrance (why?!), rendering it impassable.)

Answer: No one.

I am an able-bodied and sighted person. What if you *aren't*?
What if you have a familiar, reliable path and then one day
there's just a concrete wall there? And there's no one around to
ask where you can move safely? Or it's an active construction
site and you can't hear and are even more disoriented by the

cacophony? How do you sort it? And then how do you sort it when they knock the building across the street down? Who tells you when it's all OK again? Will you even be here?

It's outlandish to me that in the name of progress and the future, present-day life must be actively disrupted and/or grind to a fucking halt. Halifax's problem is that it's never been happy with the people who live here, it's never enough to reward the people who are already scratching it out in an overpriced, underpaid place that's not very progressive and only cares about you once you leave. It's who can we attract who has more money, more to invest, who comes from a higher tax bracket—in short, is *better*? Fuck all you peasants *walking around*, where's your car, loser? Why aren't you driving to Costco with all the other winners?

I know this is an overreaction. They're short blocks, just walk around! But it's not the inconvenience of the moment— well, not always—it's the fact that nobody *cares* in the first place. Buildings and cars always take precedence over people, and the city isn't even *nice* about it. And it's constant—it's not one street or one block or concentrated anywhere. It's city-wide and it's all like this. It's full-on disdainful, disrespectful, and disgusting.

The building is the inconvenience. The construction workers are the inconvenience. The developer is the inconvenience. You assholes can use the other side, I'm gonna walk where I want.

I HAVE THOUGHTS

THIS IS NOT A DRIVER'S LICENCE

A hallmark characteristic of queer people is a lot of us can't drive. I have no idea why, or even if there is any data to back this up, it's just a thing I believe because I heard it once and it seems to be true. (This is how you become QAnon.) Too busy flouncing around major cities with decent public transportation? That's certainly not my excuse—Halifax, despite being mid-sized at absolute best, has, in my estimation, one of the worst public transit systems in North America.

Growing up rural, all you want is your driver's licence. It's literally your only ticket out. Six months before your birthday you get "the book" from someone older than you, then you go and get your "beginner's" on your sixteenth birthday, and then a few months later you do the road test and get your licence and now you can drive everyone to the Big Stop and, one day when you're allowed on the highway, to the movies in Bedford!

When your favourite movie is *Thelma & Louise*, all you do is dream about the murderous road trips you'll take once you graduate from high school. You'll drive across America! You'll take 35mm photos! You won't ever be worried about rape or robbery because that was a movie, not real life, which as far as you know is fair and good and safe!

Except what if your anxiety about being judged live for something you're not that good at ruins this dream not once but *thrice*? And then you move to the city, which at least has *some* buses—versus your no buses at home—and you give up, and you go to the DMV when your last sad beginner's expires and you get an Identification Card and you hope they'll mess up and forget to put this part on, in red block letters, but they never do: THIS IS NOT A DRIVER'S LICENCE.

At some point in the past twenty-five years they changed that line to simply "Identification Card," in tiny black letters, and I know this because I'm in my forties and I still can't drive. Partly this doesn't matter and has never mattered because I have never been and likely will never be able to afford a car. Or if I had, I would have ended up living in it in 2009 when the economy collapsed, and I would have died.

But I have been in two bands that toured, and on a number of road trips to the US and central Canada. I don't see very well or have a good sense of direction (if we get lost in the woods together, I'm sorry to tell you the Blair Witch is gonna get us), so also being unable to legally pilot the vehicle toward its destination makes me 100 percent useless in these endeavours. Thank god I'm funny or no one would let me do anything fun!

My being able to drive would have mattered then.

It also would have mattered on any number of Thursdays— seriously I could not count them, there were so many—when the taxi to my weekly CBC hit would take up to half an hour to arrive. The radio station was in downtown Halifax for decades—the historic building was eventually knocked down for a new YMCA—but then some boneheads moved it out by the Walmart in the suburban west end. It's a terrible studio in every way—surrounded by open-concept office space (the worst corporate invention in modern times), fluorescent lighting, and terribly constructed sound studios, which would be fine if it were not the biggest eastern branch of THE NATIONAL BROADCASTER.

Anyway, it took me fifteen minutes to walk around Citadel Hill to do my weekly hits. When the studio moved in 2015 my choices became: a forty-five-minute walk (meaning I would have to leave my house at 7:00 A.M.; file that under No One Is Paying Me Enough); a ten-minute walk and five-minute bus, but all three buses came within two minutes of each other—or might never come (too stressful); or a taxi straight from my house to the studio, all of an eight-minute drive.

There are a handful of cab companies in Halifax, but the two most popular are Casino Taxi and Yellow Cab. Casino is the main one; you only call Yellow if you can't get through to Casino. Also, Casino has a famous jingle that any Haligonian can sing on demand. I can't say that isn't the main reason for its popularity because it certainly isn't its dependability.

Taxis in Halifax literally didn't get good until the pandemic (same as food and grocery delivery. This is the kind of town it is, dragging its ass for years, until it can't by default), when Casino bought Uber's technology and got a decent app.

Drivers do not turn the lights off when there's a fare in the car or on when there's not—they're permanently on, so you literally have to wait until you can see into the car to know whether it's free or not.

If there's even a hint of inclement weather, you're totally fucked.

If it's clear and sunny, you're totally fucked.

I have literally lost work because of taxis in Halifax. If I didn't make it to the studio, I didn't make it on the radio, and I didn't get paid.

The day of my last show with Don Connolly on *Information Morning*, a cold but snow-free late January day, I was still standing on my street at 8:00 A.M., the time I was due in the studio. I'd been calling Casino and giving them the same address every week for five years straight, and of course this was the week they typed it in wrong. Did anyone call me to ask where I was? Of course not. (I actually think arriving fifteen minutes late in a hot panicked rage is the reason I didn't cry during the show. But I'm not going to thank anyone for it!) That's the other thing Halifax taxi drivers do—drive off because they've gone to the wrong place and blame it on you. Their only job is to pick people up at one place and take them to another place, and it does not matter to them if it happens or not. It's truly astonishing. And I haven't even mentioned all the sexual assaults yet!

But this essay isn't about serial rapist taxi drivers, it's about how I am unable to drive myself anywhere. No, I would never be able to own a car, but I could...borrow someone's? Or, in recent years, walk to a nearby neighbourhood car share? Same goes for cat emergencies, or can't-miss appointments when it's pouring, or trying to get to the liquor store before it closes.

Not driving has also made cars as a concept completely foreign to me. I do not know models. I *might* know the colour. If I've been in your car ten times I still only know it's you when you look me in the face from the driver's seat directly in front of my house. If I were the witness in a murder and the key piece of evidence was me knowing what kind of car was involved, that murder would go unsolved. I've gotten in the passenger side of many a wrong car in parking lots. I do not give a fuck about the price of gas and I don't think they should say it on the radio—no one has ever stopped driving because of it, and actually it's one of the cheapest things you can buy on a per-unit basis, you (not I!) just need so much, all the time. Please don't talk to me about Halifax's winter parking ban, it affects my life zero percent.

Not having a driver's licence used to be a source of shame for me, but now I use it to be snooty about my carbon footprint. I have also seen friends get their licences late in life and then become "car people" who start driving really short distances and leave at the latest possible moment because they don't have to consider how long it takes to walk anymore, and they text five minutes before we're supposed to meet that they'll be fifteen minutes late but I left my house half an hour ago and I'm already here.

I do regret it sometimes. When I'm on a road trip, being dead weight, my vote counts the least. When I'm on tour in Moncton on a Thursday and there's nothing to do, I can't take the van anywhere. When it's a beautiful fall day, I can't grab a coffee and head to the sea (despite being on a peninsula, you cannot take the bus to any beach in the Halifax Regional Municipality!). When I'm sad, which is often, I can't drive around scream-singing ballads.

There are pros and cons to everything. A friend of mine has an excellent story in which she gets her licence suddenly and quickly in a snowstorm at thirty-five, and now she's a total car person and it's pretty impressive. I think I would take the test better at this age because I know what matters, and this ain't it. Occasionally some other walkers my age try to corral us all into a driver's ed group, which I do think would be hilarious and worth it, but it's too expensive and I never do it. Maybe someday I'll have a windfall for such luxuries and I will.

Until then, I'll still have to get someone to drive me to the DMV once every five years to renew my Not A Driver's Licence.

CONFESSIONS OF
A QUICK-WITTED NIHILIST

To my father, best friend, and anyone who thinks life can change because of a positive attitude:

This is the truth, and you hate when I say it: I would rather not be here.

Now, this is not to say I'm suicidal. (It's also not to say I have never been suicidal.)[1] But in general when I talk about this, I don't mean I wish I was dead. I don't have suicidal ideation. I'm not obsessed with ways to do it. I don't think about what I would write in my note.

But I do riff on it, a lot. And that bothers you. You used to let it go by but you don't anymore, now that we're older and have suffered the cumulative hardships of people our age. Pain on pain. To joke about it is frivolous and ungrateful, considering. Once at a low point in the pandemic I made some friends share how they would kill themselves and when we relayed this story to you, you did not laugh.

You've asked me to stop making suicide jokes and I have, because it makes you feel bad. But you don't realize how suicide

---

1 But if you are suicidal, there are resources. You can call this number: 1-833-456-4566 and speak to someone.

jokes are a coping mechanism for me and by taking that away you make me feel bad.

I have been lucky, I've only lost a handful of people (and two cats) in my lifetime, and none of those losses were self-inflicted. I know people who have lost loved ones in that way, and I can't fathom it. I can't imagine the guilt and confusion and rage those left behind feel. (When I occasionally do think about how I would do it, I try to picture something that involves no one having to find me. It's not possible, and it's one of the things that keeps me here.) And when I joke about walking into the sea or hoping the earth burns down before I'm fifty, I do not disrespect the losses of others, and I am not making light of them.

It probably doesn't come off that way.

The meaning of life does not exist. No one asks to be born and no one gets to pick the circumstances they're born into. As I like to say, every baby I know is richer than me. (They are your babies, by the way.) Life is what you make it, sure, but not everyone gets the same supplies. And not everyone wants to make a life.

Against most standards, mine is good. White, Canadian, middle-class, able. That's a pretty good pile to step into in the first place. My career is not well-paying but it's in the arts. I get to make records and movies and this book. I have a nice apartment (with second-hand everything). I can buy plane tickets (domestic). I can afford $9 for a single beer, even though I wish I wouldn't agree to pay that much. Culture remains reasonably priced and plentiful. When awful things have happened to me, including death, friends and family have shown up with care and whatever I needed whether I was able to ask for it or not.

So what's my fucking problem, you may be wondering?

The best way to explain it came out of a text exchange I had with a friend in fall 2021. Our bands had been planning to play a show together and then there was a minor Covid spike, so a guy in his band—who'd beaten cancer and now had a baby—backed out. I understood and didn't harp on it, but by this fully vaccinated, masked-up point I was over being worried about Covid. (I was texting him from New York City, which at the time was reporting a thousand new cases a day.)

Me: I don't value my life that much. But I appreciate those who do!

Friend: LOL OMG MAYBE THAT'S WHY I'M OK WITH DOING SHIT

That's what it comes down to. I am not stoked to be here, I did not sign up for this, and no one asked me—but I'm here, so I'm doing it.

However: I will not struggle to stay. If there's a zombie apocalypse, a tidal wave in Halifax Harbour, or some sort of military action, I will not run. I will not climb to the highest elevation or take refuge underground. I will not save anyone, I will not fight a monster, I will not rebuild.

I know it's hard not to take this attitude personally, but I'm not going to pretend to love it here just to give you one less thing to worry about. We live in a rich, democratic country, and I have the freedom to think what I want about any damn thing. And I think life is more bad than good. I would rather not be here.

With apologies, and no regrets,
Thorney

I GOT ENDED

Stephen McNeil was the twenty-eighth premier of Nova Scotia and he governed for two terms, beginning in 2013. A Conservative in a red tie, across those eight years he habitually made life worse for teachers, nurses, arts workers, and the media.

Not long before the second election, the premier's adult son moved in with my downstairs neighbour. I had no relationship with her other than to say hi on the stoop, but she seemed nice enough. They met at Irving, and I don't mean a gas station—in their respective jobs at the Irving Shipyard, which continues to get millions of dollars for various projects that have yet to happen (ships start where, exactly?), and attempted to skirt the province's intense Covid rules at the height of the pandemic. Just so we're all aware of the layers here.

The son drove a giant truck that took up two parking spots on our permit-only block; it was the kind of truck someone who went out to Fort McMurray to work in the patch would have spent fifty grand on and driven back. I called it The Chode Truck—because only a chode would drive a truck like that—which became me and my then-roommate naming them, as a couple,

The Chodes. They were in their mid-twenties, generically attractive, and basic as hell. They drank Bud Light, watched only explodey action movies, and listened to Ed Sheeran on purpose.

The house I lived in was lovely and divided into two flats: Upstairs was two bedrooms, downstairs was one, and my two were overtop the bottom one. The Chodes had sex every single day, sometimes more than once. I know this because I heard it, thanks to the great mystery of some engineering defect, every single time. Worse: it always happened the same way. It was like listening to someone watch the same porn to go to sleep, but with the added horror of knowing it was actually happening. It sounded like a put-on performance, cranked to a hundred from the beginning.

I often thought, while waiting for sleep to take me away, about how sad it was that they'd likely learned about sex from porn, given their ages. (I feel the same way when I watch *Euphoria*.) I joked about leaving a copy of *Girlsex 101* at their door so he could mix it up. My friends at work encouraged me to write a Fringe show about it (imagine!), that's how much I talked about it.

A year or two later they bought a starter condo in West Bedford or whatever it is people like them do, someone else moved in downstairs, and I never thought about them again until August 6, 2020.

*

My entry into CBC life set the tone for its exit but I, too, was once a young basic bitch and that was exactly when my boss at *The Coast* took me out to lunch and pitched me the idea that I would go onto the Halifax station's flagship radio show weekly and tell them about "what was going on" from a young, alternative person's perspective. (*Information Morning*'s mean listener age is in their fifties.) He did not tell me at that meeting—and to be fair to him, the man who would go on to fuck me around about money for another fifteen years, I did not ask—that it was a volunteer position.

Let me stop right here to confirm what you're wondering: No, CBC is not supposed to do that.

The day before I was set to appear for the first time I asked the producer if I could try one out, see if it worked, and then I would decide. She said no, she didn't want to set the audience up to expect me then have it go away. (Dear GOD, the bullshit I have taken from higher-ups my entire life.) Everyone around me was sure this was my big break, and all the advice I was getting said to do it, and I've never been good at believing my own feelings—and back then I really wasn't—so I did it.

And something unexpected happened: I hit it off with the host. I've made a movie and I know this to be an absolute—you cannot buy or teach or fake chemistry. It's there or it's not. And with us, it was there. He was a good thirty years older, he called me Kid—it probably reads condescendingly if you haven't heard it, but it wasn't—and he was a local institution who'd been on the air for decades. He loved to talk to me. I loved to talk to him. It was gently ribbing, piss-taking, funny, and affectionate. Listeners loved us together (except for the ones who thought I talked too fast). People didn't care about my information, they cared about the relationship.

I had a bargaining chip.

Six months in, I made a case for myself to the producer. She said she was "disappointed," classic Mom shit, but agreed to pay me the absolute bare minimum as dictated by the union that governed her workplace. (We'll get to grievances later, but I had one from the jump.)

I don't need a whole hand to count the number of spots I missed from 2004 to 2020. I had Norovirus one week; somebody died another. When I went to the Toronto International Film Festival every year I recorded from a closet in the big national broadcast centre. If I took a vacation I worked the dates around being in Halifax on Thursdays (then Fridays, and then back to Thursdays). If that wasn't possible, we pre-recorded and hoped no breaking arts news happened. (It...didn't.)

I set an alarm clock and my phone alarm every week, because the power goes out a lot here, and never needed the backup. I refused to drink even one alcohol the night before a show, that's how afraid I was of sleeping through my alarm(s). Many times I dragged ass to the studio half-sick—because if you don't do the hit you don't get paid—or absolutely fucking bereft about girl or work troubles, and you would never have known. Occasionally I said names that were sawdust in my mouth, of musicians and actors and artists, and you couldn't tell how much it hurt.

Once there was a fire alarm during the show and we did a hit from the Public Gardens. Once I slipped on ice walking in and split my pants up the middle and didn't have time to walk home and did the hit with my coat draped over my lower half. Once I played Santa in a sketch for the annual food bank show and kicked into Madonna's version of "Santa Baby" and the live audience did golf claps. When the host retired, I wrote him a song and sang it live on the air.

I was part of it, you know? Those 8 minutes a week (which became 18 once I signed on as the film critic for the morning radio shows in Saint John and Moncton) were a huge chunk of my identity. For fifteen years, across three cities, I was in it.

*

Nova Scotia is an uptight, rule-abiding place, so of course our time to shine was in a worldwide pandemic. Lockdown, widely available free testing, and a general distrust of our neighbours—the perfect combination with which to beat this fucker.

Dr. Robert Strang was the chief medical officer of health for the province and, unlike Stephen McNeil, was effective and well-liked. Strang had had this job since 2007—he was a pre-Covid CBC guest often, in fact—but the Nova Scotia public only really became aware of his power in the pandemic. During the first lockdown it became a ritual to watch Strang's daily press conference on YouTube—case counts, new information, restrictions. McNeil would sit next to him and people, with few options for fresh entertainment, really dug into their Good Cop/Bad Cop vibe. (You know who's who.)

Six months into the pandemic, sitting in an essentially reopened Nova Scotia—this would, of course, change—McNeil made a surprise announcement: He was ejecting, leaving the premier's job six months early. Even though, for once in his life, he'd done a good job.

It was August and we were in a heat wave, so my air conditioner (for once, I had one!) was blaring ineffectively behind me while I worked remotely in admin for an arts festival. The news that the premier had quit ripped through the office Slack, then we all went for lunch. Natasha Pace, an excellent reporter for CTV Atlantic (so sorry, Natasha), tweeted:

> McNeil says his wife, Andrea, has been amazing. He says she probably felt like a single parent a lot of the time. He says his children were young when he went into politics, he says it's been hard for his kids to hear the negative comments while he has been in politics

Did you know the premier of Nova Scotia, a largely useless skin tag on the side of this country, is the third highest-paid premier in Canada? Think about that through the rest of this.

The thing about tweeting is people who don't use the internet treat it like it's a six-month reported investigative longread, but only when it matters to them. I have written more than FIFTY THOUSAND tweets in eleven years. Is this a worthy way to spend one's life? Obviously not. But it's what I've done. I hit Quote Tweet on Natasha's post and number forty-eight-thousand-and-something was this:

> It was hard for me to hear his son bang my downstairs neighbour the exact same way every night, life is hard

Two things happened: I worried that I had gone too far, and this tweet went off.

I asked a couple journalist friends if it was too much; they thought it was funny and if the network didn't like it, they were uptight dorks. A CBC friend in another part of the country called: "Can we talk about how much I love your tweet?" I made a joke about how I was heat-raged and that would be my defense when they called to fire me. People online continued to respond in a favourable fashion. The next morning I had a meeting and the air was cool in the shade for the first time in weeks. I went to someone's yard and drank coffee and ate croissants and talked about the movie I'd written and would direct that I'd received Telefilm funding for. It would be announced the following week.

When I got home I had an email from the producer of the show. He was filling in for the vacationing producer and—as both a cause and effect of this situation across my career—nothing sucks more than having to deal with a real problem when you're in a temporary job. He said a lady had emailed him angry about my tweet and even though I had more latitude than a full-time employee, would I take it down.

Immediately I bristled—nobody at any job, now or ever, paid me enough to censor me. I called my life coach and asked her what I should do. She was completely unaware of any of it and I could hear her mood shift live on the phone as she dug into it. A failed politician who'd had his own blackface scandal during which he cried while not-really apologizing had taken a screenshot of the tweet, posted it to Facebook, and sent the Liberal toadies to my open account. The people who'd found it funny twenty-four hours previous had been pushed down the timeline by faux outrage from old south-enders and brand-new accounts with egg avatars and handles made of numbers.

I called the producer—at this point, I was still amused. He said more had happened since he emailed me; a lady had called the station and said she "didn't want Tara Thorne to get fired," but....

He was laughing nervously and somehow I didn't catch on, thanked me for taking the tweet down and replacing it with some kind of apology, and then he said something that would become important by end of day: "Ken saw it, and he thought it was funny, but he's looking at the freelancer code of conduct in the Journalistic Standards and Practices."

One: Ken Macintosh is the executive producer of news and current affairs at CBC Halifax, so if you're mad enough at someone and you come from the right neighbourhood, it gets to him. We only ever said hi in the mornings when I passed his desk as I was leaving the studio, we'd never worked together or had any conversations of note. The JSP is the governing principle of the network, and in my fifteen years there, on three different shows and multiple freelance appearances including a two-year stint on *Q*—a national show and a network flagship—I was never given or pointed to them.

Two: I've been on Twitter since 2010, and I tweet with abandon. I swear, I subtweet, I talk about whatever I want. That's always been true. Not once in the ten concurrent years that I was on Twitter and CBC did a producer or host ever flag a tweet, or warn me about my conduct on the platform, or ask me to take anything down. Nobody else from CBC ever even DM'd me to say, "Hey, you should know this is ruffling feathers in the office," nothing. Nobody noticed, nobody cared.

Three: I am a rule follower and moralistic to my own detriment. If at any point I had been given a document to read I would have not just read it, I would have internalized it totally, and followed its instructions fully. If at any point someone had chastised me, I would have listened, because I need money more than I need to tweet.

At 5:00 P.M. that Friday, I got a call from Ken. He looped in Meredith Dellandrea, an executive in Montreal who was also responsible for the Atlantic region. She had never heard of me before that day.

To my surprise, I was defensive to the point of petulance. I'd spent my whole life kowtowing to people who didn't respect me or deserve it in return but in 2019, in my final days at *The Coast*, I'd decided I'd had enough of that shit. I immediately asked Meredith if I needed a union representative on the call—I had just, two weeks previous and after six months of trying, become a member of the Canadian Media Guild in an attempt to get affordable health insurance—and she said no, "as a freelance columnist, you don't need a union rep."

It did not go well from there.

From my notes for the union rep I absolutely did need and got the next day, a Saturday:

> *Meredith told me this was serious, that the tweet did not meet the standards of journalistic practices for CBC, and now they had to re-evaluate their business relationship with me because I had jeopardized the CBC's "business partnership" (her words) with the province of Nova Scotia.*
>
> *Ken added that the network needed to keep that relationship viable because the premier is in office until next year.*

I worked at The Coast for twenty years and I have heard and handled my fair share of angry advertisers—based on those statements, at this point I began to suspect the premier's office ran this up the chain at CBC.

I also said to Ken, "I've been tweeting negatively about the premier all through the pandemic" and his response was "I don't follow you." I have been on air with Info AM Halifax for fifteen-plus years and I have never been given or directed to standards and practices, nor a freelancer online code of conduct. Ken said, "Well you should have." (I've been with Info AM since before Twitter was invented.)

Meredith asked me to draft an apology and send it to communications and CC her. I was initially against apologizing but relented in the end, asking if I apologized could I still be off the show and Meredith said yes. I asked who was doing the internal review and she said she was when I asked if [my producer] would be involved she said no, "This is a business decision, not an editorial decision." She would tell me the decision on Monday.

For those of you who know about Freedom of Information requests, know this: The apology was the only thing that ever happened over email. Everything else was a phone call or text, including the meetings local execs held with (actual) employees who'd emailed them in disappointment or anger about my dismissal in the wake of it all. And they did that because you can FOIPOP an email.

This was my bullshit apology draft I sent deep into Friday
night:

*I apologize to the premier's son for tweeting about his
personal life; as a private citizen he's not open to the same
scrutiny as his father and it wasn't fair. I also apologize
to my colleagues at CBC, who work diligently and with
dignity to keep the press fair and balanced.*

The communications person had a single edit: She asked
me to change "my colleagues" to "the team," and I knew then I
was done.

*

They don't call it "fired" or "terminated." Because I didn't technically work there, I couldn't be fired. Even after a decade and a
half of being paid by CBC in two provinces, plus a smattering of
national work. There was a business relationship, and there was
ending the business relationship.

So I didn't get fired. I got ended.

*

It happened on Monday afternoon, the air heavy with humidity
and dread. It took six minutes. Meredith texted to set up the
meeting, then called. She once again denied me union rep-
resentation, confirmed that I was being ended for a single tweet,
asked me if I had any questions for the HR guy (no) also on the
line, and thanked me for my work. (I have not yet gotten over
how she thanked me for my work.)

The next few days were a blur. I deleted Twitter entirely, took a screenshot of the deletion and put it in an Instagram story. Friends picked up on it instantly and went in on Twitter themselves. News ripped around town. People were saying very nice things about me and my career, but every time I followed a link someone sent I saw something horrible, so I stopped looking. I laid in bed and wept. The retired host called me, a true kindness. People from the station sent me support from their Gmails—remember, CBC emails are FOIPOPable; *my* Gmail thought I was the target of multiple phishing scams—or DM'd me on Messenger.

It felt like I was watching my own funeral.

I received two bouquets that were, in a plot twist that could only happen in this fucking town, delivered by a CBC employee who was on vacation and helping out at his wife's flower shop. I called the New Brunswick hosts, who had no idea what was happening or what it had to do with their stations or province. One of the Halifax hosts was on vacation but I connected with the other and apologized, through copious tears, for embarrassing her. I talked to the president of the Canadian Media Guild. I exchanged emails with Jesse Brown, the rich-guy rabble-rouser who runs the news site *Canadaland*. I talked to the lawyer Ron Pink, who jokingly yelled at me for signing such a shitty contract, as if it had ever been up to me.

Two of my best friends took me to Conrad's Beach and I posted an Instagram series joking about walking into the sea—a joke I have made a lot, for a long time—but being unable to find it because it was low tide and so foggy. (It was so foggy, in fact, that we couldn't find the exit and had to map ourselves on our phones so the GPS could show us.) When we finally got back to the car, I had three messages asking if I needed help.

I mean, they were right to be worried. I had to repeatedly tell strangers at the union or in a law office my story, this ridiculous fucking tweet that was still getting daylighted and willfully misconstrued. Death would have been a sweet relief from that embarrassment.

But we got back in the car and went to Dairy Queen, and the next day I delivered a bio to Telefilm—cheerily requested by a stranger excited on my behalf—so they could announce my film.

It began: "Tara Thorne is a recovering journalist."

*

If you've flipped directly to this essay then you might not know this, but really if you have any idea about me you should know that I do not care about what happens to straight white men. Their time is over. Do I feel bad about what I tweeted, specifically? Absolutely not. If it had been just a random man's son, no one would have ever cared; if the Liberal toadies had thought it through they would have realized pointing it out only extends its life not just to do harm to me, but also to expand the alleged embarrassment the premier's son felt—that is, if you believe men can be slut-shamed, which I don't. Some people pretended to seriously ask what if it were his daughter (it wasn't), or what if I were a male journalist (I'm not) tweeting about a woman (it was a man), or did I think about his girlfriend at all (I identified her as "my downstairs neighbour" only, no gender, cool assumption). I wanted more for his girlfriend, that was the fucking point!

Do I regret the tweet? Yes and no. Yes, because I knew immediately that a line had been crossed, but I knew it was funny and I wanted the external validation. I regret that I needed that. I regret that it made everyone else I worked with at the time feel like it was necessary to hold meetings to decide whether they could continue working with me. And I regret that I no longer get to speak with the hosts and techs I loved working with, and that we'll never get a goodbye. Occasionally a random person will recognize me by voice and say something like, "Love listening to you on Thursdays!" and I just let them have it, because they're clearly not a regular listener and will never know the difference.

I got ended on August 10, 2020. By Labour Day, I had my first feature film fully funded by Telefilm, a podcast with the *Halifax Examiner*, and a deal for this book with Nimbus. It turns out the corporation was dark energy holding me back from my destiny and I'd had no idea. I would have stayed on until I aged out, which in CBC time means I would have been on the air into my fifties.

It's certainly not the way I would have chosen to go. I've spent many nights falling asleep to my own various quitting fantasies over the years. We've all dreamed of standing up and walking out in a big dramatic fashion, a story that becomes company lore or at least a party anecdote, but this was not that. No matter how well things have turned out since, if not for this I never would have quit. They would have had to ask me to leave and they would have been kind about it, some bullshit about budget probably, and I would have had my little goodbye week with a cake and people calling in and we all would have moved on as friends.

But I didn't want to quit. I'd never considered it, why would I? And on that day in August I was just living a tacky old regular afternoon, taking a swing at our bad premier, like I'd done many times before. The tweet was not me taking a moral stance, or standing up for what I believe in, or doing something brave. I made a dumb joke about a rich kid and the institution—the same one that let Jian Ghomeshi maraud around for years causing actual harm to his actual co-workers until it was forced into accountability by the public it serves—let me fall to the ground. (I lost five figures, in a pandemic.)

Many people from inside the network showed up for me, and I can't even thank them because to name them would threaten their own careers. There are ones I could name, higher up, who failed me and didn't apologize. This is a small town, we see each other often. (There's a Winners out by the studio.) They duck their heads and offer wan smiles like somebody just died.

The same week I got ended my band began recording an EP. The project had been delayed from the winter and the dates were booked for months—it was nice to have the distraction, although in retrospect it was not great planning. (I had to re-record all my guitars because my playing was clenched and off-putting, wonder why.) We'd blocked off the entire weekend to make it, so I was out of the house for eight to ten hours a day, away from the relentless online chatter, and I was grateful to be with kind, funny, talented friends who supported me, and make music with them.

When I walked out of the studio on Sunday evening, the air had turned crisp and autumnal, the kind of freshness that always fills me with hope whenever it starts blowing at the end of a long summer. (This had been the longest summer.) It felt like a gift just for me, and for the first time in nearly ten straight days of nerve-rattling turmoil I felt like I might be okay.

This was the first record I'd gotten to use my St. Vincent guitar on and I walked home with it on my back as the sun set. When I arrived, tucked into the corner of my stoop was a vase holding fifteen roses—not quite pink, not quite orange, incredibly dazzling. It was a beautiful arrangement with no flower shop paper; someone had dropped them off personally. A torn-off, folded square of paper formed the handmade card, which had *FOR TARA* written in ballpoint pen on the front.

There was no signature inside (to this day I don't know who this bouquet was from; if it was you, please tell me now). But there were six words, underlined with a zigzag flourish:

FUCK CBC, MAKE YOUR OWN ART

LOW ROAD FOREVER

There's a common saying, you've heard it your whole life. As a failed English major I don't know where it comes from, and just in case it's the Bible I'm not going to look it up. But here it is:

Take the high road.

What this means is: Be classy. Don't cause a fuss. Stay quiet. Do the right thing.

Here's my concern: Who is deciding what the right thing is? Who defines class? Who is telling you to shut up?

The older I get—I'm also not going to look up how many times I've used that phrase in this humble tome—the more I realize how many rules are in place to keep the peace for a certain kind of person. That person is in charge, is unlikely to have earned it honestly, and doesn't want to deal with unrest because it's difficult and inconvenient. So...your parents. A boss. Elon Musk. People in power positions.

When someone says to you, "You should take the high road," what they are saying is You should shut the fuck up and stop causing trouble. Shame is a mighty powerful tool—my favourite advice columnist, Heather Havrilesky, a.k.a. Ask Polly, points to shame as the root of most issues—so by flipping a situation back on you and making it seem as if standing up for yourself or fighting back is not a demonstration of integrity and self-assurance but an embarrassment, the powers that be are keeping you compliant and silent.

By keeping you in check, they grow their power. And most importantly, their own terrible, truly shameful behaviour and actions continue to go buried and uncommented-upon. Shame and fear are at the core of maintaining all power structures.

The power structure known as the patriarchy covers dating—it's not all jobs and death in here—and it is often in relationship situations that you hear "Take the high road." And that's because women, in particular, are so easily and thoughtlessly dismissed as unwell and unhinged that they are shamed into not expressing their feelings so no one will call them "crazy." (Many more thoughts on this can be found on page 84.)

Take the high road! And push your trauma down so far that it will affect you for the rest of your life. Take the high road! And let the other person walk away unscathed and damage someone else with their shitty behaviour. Take the high road! So that man doesn't have to look inward, ever. Take the high road! Because crying is how she gets out of talking about anything important.

Disrespectfully, fuck that. (While we're here, I also do not wish you well. See you in hell.)

If you google "Take the high road" lots of stuff comes up, but here are some of the most commonly appearing, and why they're lies (caveat: I have no idea of the context for any of them, and context is important, but hopefully we'll all learn something about using this phrase at all):

"Disciplining yourself to do what you know is right and
important, although difficult, is the high road to pride,
self-esteem, and personal satisfaction."
—Margaret Thatcher

Okay the first one was a joke.

"Love is a helium-based emotion; love always takes the
high road."
—Augusten Burroughs

Augusten Burroughs is an author but before that he was an
advertising guy, so I don't want to hear it from him. Love will
step over any relationship, child, geographical boundary, job
promotion, flightpath, or declaration of intention if it feels like it.

"Take the high road. No matter how much strife, and
consternation, frustration and anger you might be
confronted with—don't go to that level."
—Tim Gunn

Tim Gunn is a fashion person and a delight, but that industry is amoral. Between the high-class pissing matches, favour-
trading, and deal-making among designers, models, magazine
editors, and sundry rich people, there's just no way that he
actually believes in the high road. You think you get your own
TV show from up in the sky? No no, you dig your *Project Runway*
out of the dirt.

> "Sometimes—this is a tough one—not everyone can
> handle the truth. Sometimes you have to take a beat.
> But if you can take that beat, and take the high road, it'll
> serve you in the long run."
> —Jeremy Piven

Jeremy Piven is an actor and known douchebag who lied about having mercury poisoning so he could quit a Broadway show. He also award-winningly portrayed the brash and successful Hollywood agent Ari Gold on *Entourage,* and that's another world where the high road literally doesn't exist. I suspect he was defending his sushi lie with this quote, and the people who collect memes should know better about him.

> "Take the high road; it's far less crowded."
> —Warren Buffett

Warren Buffett is a billionaire who made his money in investing, but people like him because he's from Nebraska and has given away billions of dollars of that cash. As of this writing public opinion has largely shifted to an understanding that as a concept billionaires should not exist. Warren's road is uncrowded because no one but Bill Gates even knows where it is.

> "What is the use of living, if it be not to strive for noble
> causes and to make this muddled world a better place
> for those who will live in it after we are gone? How else
> can we put ourselves in harmonious relation with the

great verities and consolations of the infinite and the
eternal? And I avow my faith that we are marching
towards better days. Humanity will not be cast down. We
are going on swinging bravely forward along the grand
high road and already behind the distant mountains is
the promise of the sun."
—Winston Churchill

Winston Churchill was the prime minister of England and
he said this in 1908 in Scotland about god knows what when he
was the president of the Board of Trade. We all know England's
history and there are no high roads to be found there. In 2018,
known wife-beater Gary Oldman was given the Academy Award
for Best Actor for his portrayal of Churchill in *Darkest Hour*, a
long and boring film I do not recommend.

"Those who travel the high road of humility are not
troubled by heavy traffic."
—Alan K. Simpson

Alan K. Simpson is a former senator from Wyoming, known
for its vast expanses of humility. As a member of the Republican
party, however, he does not get to speak of the high road.

Humility, too, is seen as a positive trait because it's the
opposite of arrogance. But its synonyms don't come with its
folksy elegance: docile, timid, meek, subservient. To praise
humility is to merely shut down a problem. It's a trick!

"Pray for the strength to walk the high road, which at
times may be lonely but which will lead to peace and
happiness and joy supernal."
—Gordon B. Hinckley

Gordon B. Hinckley was a Mormon from Salt Lake City who
was the president of the Church of Jesus Christ of Latter-day
Saints. No one in any power position at any church can claim
humility, and like all major religious sects, the LDS has covered
up sexual abuse throughout its existence, including of ninety
thousand Boy Scouts of America. Gordon is not living in peace
supernal.

"The high road is always respected. Honesty and
integrity are always rewarded."
—Scott Hamilton

Scott Hamilton is an Olympic gold medalist in figure skat-
ing; he beat cancer and he seems nice, but honesty and integrity
are often fighting a losing battle against manipulation and lies.
That always is doing a lot of work.

"The high road's the only road I know. Let's keep on that
way."
—Jim Harbaugh

Jim Harbaugh is a coach in one of the most corrupt systems
in America, college football. One of my favourite episodes of

TARA THORNE

Friday Night Lights is in the misunderstood fourth season when they introduced East Dillon, a shitty high school with a worse football team, Coach Taylor's worst nightmare (of course he ended up coaching there). And World's Best Woman Tami Taylor learned that there was a mailbox in a field that parents in East Dillon had been using as a fake address in Dillon proper for years so their football sons could technically attend Dillon High School, and she also learned Coach knew about the mailbox and she gave him what for. And then she walked out onto the field during practice, in the rain, in front of her own damn husband, and told Luke—who lived with his grandma in East Dillon—he had to change schools and he cried. And then apologized to lying to her even though it wasn't his lie, not at the start. Tami Taylor may be the only person who actually knows what the high road is.

I worked for two companies for most of my adult life and they both pulled some shit, much of it too uninteresting to explain. But one time, early on, it was a co-pro: CBC didn't pay me for the first ten months I was a weekly on-air columnist because I was getting a weekly blast of that thing you can't eat or pay bills with, exposure, and it was *The Coast* who offered me to the show for free in the first place. CBC got to do a segment for young people, the paper got mentioned on the radio, so everyone won but me, who literally could not afford a cab from my home around Citadel Hill to the radio studio most weeks (and it rained every Thursday—my day on the show—that first year).

A dozen years later a CBC producer tried to coerce me into submitting a written version of my audio column without any additional compensation. On the phone, my point person on the show asked me if fighting it was "The hill [I] wanted to die on."

After years of doing the exact same job with no advancement and realizing I was doing all they thought I could, I knew there was no threat. Or I was at least willing to accept the fallout. "It's the only hill I have," I replied. (I refused to do the extra work and the whole idea was dropped.)

I have learned the hard way that the high road is a fraud, an illusion, a basic concept for fairy tales about good and evil and nothing more. Real life is too nuanced and complicated for such a clear-cut distinction. And yes, there is a great class divide that, in bare numbers, divides us into high and low, have and have-not. But mostly we're all fist fighting our way through the muck of the middle, trying to make life not suck. We're all bumbling around down here, making it work.

So, to every boss, family member, love interest, internet commenter, politician, or institution that's ever suggested I take the high road, I say a hearty fuck you.

Low road forever.

ACKNOWLEDGEMENTS

Thank you to Whitney Moran for being one of the kind hands who reached down and pulled me out of the muck of a terrible time. Thank you to Stephanie Domet, my first and best boss, who I've turned to on many occasions throughout my life for advice and/or an ass-kicking. If you weren't part of this, I would have abandoned it out of fear. Thank you Martha Cooley and the AFCOOP folks for letting me creep in the corner (and for asking after word counts!). Thank you to Allison Devereaux for habitually (and kindly) asking me about the progress of this project even when I was being a real dick about it. Thank you to all my friends, close and far, for your support and encouragement in a time when energy was in short supply. Thank you to every English teacher I've ever had, especially Sonya Singer and Janet Baker. And thank you to all the Coasties (2000–2019) who made me a better writer, editor, thinker, and person.

TARA THORNE has been an arts advocate and journalist in Halifax since 2000. She leads the rock band Dance Movie and coordinates the Halifax Independent Filmmakers Festival. Her feature debut as writer and director, *Compulsus,* is currently on the film-festival circuit.